YOUR FIRST SCREENPLAY

The Beginner's Guide
To Movie Writing

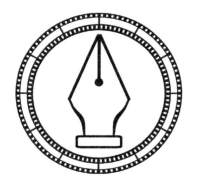

Adam Fiske

"He who jumps into the void owes no explanation to those who stand and watch."
- Jean-Luc Godard

This book is dedicated to those who jump

Contents

Chapter 1

YOU'VE COME TO THE RIGHT PLACE

Have you ever finished watching a movie and thought, *That's the best they could come up with? I could come up with a better movie idea than that.* Or you've had an idea and thought, *That would make a great movie*, but never developed it further. Maybe you've had this idea in your head for a while and just aren't sure how to get it from your mind onto the page. Perhaps you have even written down your idea, but had trouble developing it past that first step. Or have you always wanted to be a screenwriter, but the formatting, structure, and technical issues have prevented you from pursuing your dream? Well, if any of these scenarios sound familiar, you've come to the right place. I can assure you that I have personally been in every one of those situations, at one point or another, in my own screenwriting journey.

That is why I wrote this book. Through the years of developing my craft, I always found it frustrating that every time I tried to learn the next step in my process, I had to track down a new resource. Every source of information only took me so far. Formatting? Go to a class. Structure? Go to a workshop. Character? Check out this website. Dialogue? Action? Rewrites? There is so much to cover that it can seem endless. And endlessly aggravating.

Additionally, I wanted to make the process more accessible to the everyday, real person with a life outside of writing. Most resources I've come across seem to think that every burgeoning screenwriter has pledged an oath to devote every waking second to the act of writing and churning out hard-fought pages. Most people don't have that kind of time, and I understand that. This is a process that is thorough, but flexible. I've done my best to make it useful to all; from those who are dedicated to becoming professional screenwriters, to those who are interested in it as a pastime or hobby to come back to at their leisure.

I knew I had to formulate my own way of doing things. A way that worked from the start of a screenplay and would take me all the way to the end. I had to take all of those bits and pieces of knowledge and sculpt them together into a cohesive whole. After years of trial and error, reading every screenwriting book I could get my hands on, taking classes, watching instructional videos, reading screenplays, watching films, making films, talking to filmmaker colleagues, and writing, writing, writing, I was finally able to distill it all down into my own process. And that is the process I'm going to share with you.

While the task itself can be daunting, the first time you write a screenplay is immensely satisfying. Finishing each step is a victory. Each one builds on the last and culminates in the finished commodity of a feature-length script. And once written, your screenplay will be exactly that, a commodity that has value. One that you can submit to contests, agents, managers, and production companies. Given the means, you could even produce it into a film yourself. But, that is another subject for another book.

In this book, I'll walk you, step-by-step, through each part of a screenplay. From humble beginnings of finding and nurturing an idea to putting the finishing touches on your last draft. In between, you'll learn everything you need to know: finding and shaping ideas, the basics of script format, character development, using scene cards, timelines, dialogue, action, and rewrites. Once learned, all of these skills can give you the insights needed to construct a professional, polished screenplay the very first time you write one.

Honestly, this isn't the easiest process to go through. Writing a screenplay can be a rollercoaster. I guarantee you will have days where you feel like you've written poorly. But, you'll also have days where you won't believe you've written so well. At times in your screenwriting journey, you will feel tested, even frustrated. But, in my experience, that is how you know something is worth doing. If it was easy, everyone would do it. All of the ups and downs, frustrations, defeats, victories, coffee, ink, typing, feedback, critiques, rewrites, and reworking you go through will breathe life into your writing. There is no better feeling in this world than when you write the words "FADE OUT" on the last page of your screenplay. A screenplay that you created. A screenplay you put your heart and soul into. A screenplay that is yours.

A screenplay that was a journey well worth taking. I'm excited for you to get there. Thank you for choosing me as your guide.

Welcome to Your First Screenplay.

Chapter 2

WHAT YOU WILL NEED

W riting a feature length screenplay is much like going on an expedition. And, like the explorers of old, you will need some equipment before you start.

NOTE: There are digital equivalents to all of these items. For my process, analog pen and paper are preferred before I get to the first draft. Keeping things separate also helps me mentally keep track of what step in the process I am on, rather than simply opening up a laptop for every step. Additionally, a pen and paper can never freeze up, not turn on, or crash like a computer can. Also, for illustrative purposes here, listing individual items rather than different software programs can give you a clearer picture of the steps. That being said, feel free to use a laptop, tablet, or even your phone with whatever apps and programs you like. Remember, this is how *I* do it, which will help you figure out how *you* can do it.

Items You Will Need

1. **Pens (at least two).** A writer needs a good pen. Or multiple pens, in most cases. First and foremost, find one that feels comfortable in your hand. You're going to spend a lot of time holding this pen, so make sure it feels good. Next, a smooth ink flow is very important. A pen with bad flow will make you write slowly. If you write slowly, you'll be waiting for your pen to catch up to your ideas. Get one that writes smoothly. That way, your ideas can glide from your mind to your page without any hindrance. Lastly, make sure you get a box full. I go through at least two pens per screenplay. I always have more than a few extras around. You'll be surprised how fast you go through them once you get started. A pen is the writer's primary weapon, being without one is like a knight without a sword. Once you find the one you like, get plenty.

2. **Small notepads/notebooks.** You need a place to jot down ideas as they come. When an idea hits, you need to record it as quickly as possible. A small notebook or notepad that you can carry with you works best. I use a leather-bound pad like a detective or police

officer would carry. Anything small enough to carry on you will do. I like to keep several going at once. One in my writing bag, one on the nightstand (for late night ideas), and one in my pocket. It may seem like overkill, but you'd be surprised how often you have a great idea while you're not at home. Example: you're out with friends and meet an incredibly unique person and think, *I have to base a character on this person.* Then you continue your night and you don't get home until hours later. Will you still remember every single detail that made the person unique? Unlikely. If you have a notepad on hand, you can record ideas as they happen. I can't tell you how many great ideas I lost before implementing this system. You may think you can just remember it without writing it down. Unless you have an extraordinary memory, you will forget something. Avoid this by having a notepad with you.

3. **Large notepads (at least two)**. Once you have your idea quickly scribbled down, you'll need a larger pad to flesh it out in depth. Use it when you get home after your idea strikes you. This way you can use your quick notes to think more about the idea and write down anything that comes to you. These pads are perfect for that. Not too long, but a larger canvas to expand your concepts. I prefer to use the yellow legal type of pad. They are easy to find and come in multipacks. The second notepad is for your scene breakdown just before you write your rough draft. That comes later.

4. **3 x 5 index cards**. You'll need these to put down individual scene ideas. Scene ideas can come to you at any time during the process of writing a screenplay. It's important to have a way to write them quickly. But what scene cards also allow the writer to do is arrange them in any way they want. Many times, you'll think of a scene without knowing where it fits into the story. What you can do with scene cards is continually shuffle them around until the sequence of events in your script feels right. I keep stacks of these things around at all times. Much like pens, they're cheap, and you can never have too many. I like to use Sharpie markers to write my cards

out. That way, they are easy to read when putting them in order and shuffling them around.

5. **Large notebook (200+ pages).** This is to hand write your first draft. Yes, with this method, you do hand write your first draft. I know it seems tough, but there are many good reasons for it. We'll get to them later. For now, get yourself a big notebook. I like to use the spiral bound variety because they can fold down flat when writing without the previous pages flapping around. I use one that is 200 pages because my handwriting is roughly two times larger than typed. When the pages are all full, or nearly full, I know I have a script that is roughly 100 pages when it is typed up later.

6. **A laptop or PC.** So you can type up your rough draft into a first draft. Once your rough draft is complete and you've made your notes, you'll need to type it up. I like to use a laptop or tablet with a keyboard. The short keystrokes help me type faster. Use anything you like to type with, as long as you can edit it and save it as a PDF file as the final version.

7. **Screenwriting software.** Get one of these to save yourself the headache of correct formatting. Here's an open secret about screenwriters: no one knows how to properly format a script. Sure, in the early days of Hollywood, where each script was pecked out on a typewriter, a writer knowing exactly the different number of spaces for dialogue, action, scene headings, parentheticals, etc. was a requirement. Now, we just let software handle all that. Final Draft is the industry standard and the one I favor. It's fairly straightforward and easy to use. Also, most every professional screenwriter in Hollywood uses it (they advertise that some 95% of all productions are written with it). However, as of this writing, Final Draft costs $199.99. Not a very budget friendly price. If you're serious about screenwriting beyond a hobby and you have the money, it is the best of the best. If Final Draft is outside of your budget, fear not. There are plenty of other options, both paid and free. Paid programs to consider are: Write Brothers Movie Magic Screenplay ($149.99), Script Studio ($149.99), Fade In ($79.99), Arc Studio ($69/year subscription), Celtx ($15/month subscription), and

Writer Duet ($9.99/month subscription). Free options include KIT Scenarist, Trelby, and DramaQueen. This is just to name a few of many. A lot of programs boast about the features they come with (online collaboration, assignable voices, scene cards, breakdowns, reports, charts, etc.). Don't worry about what bells and whistles your program does or doesn't come with. For our purposes, simple, proper formatting is all we're looking for. All of the paid programs I've mentioned have free trial versions so you can take them for a spin with no commitment. Don't overthink it. I wrote my first screenplay on the now ancient Final Draft 4 and it still looks great and meets today's industry standards. Find a program you like and go with it. It's near impossible to get one you can't use these days.

Chapter 3

FINDING IDEAS

Okay, you've gathered your supplies. You're ready to write. But now you have to face the eternal question for all writers, "*What* do I write about?" You need an idea. And, for a feature-length screenplay, you're going to need more than one to fill things out. Even bad ideas can be tricky to come up with, and good ones can be downright elusive. So, how do you do it? The best advice I can give you is to put yourself in an ideal headspace to let the ideas come to you. In my experience, constantly banging your head against the wall (or desk, floor, laptop, etc.) is not the way to come up with viable ideas. In fact, I would go so far as to say this is the only way to ensure you *don't* come up with anything. As much as you would like to, you can't force ideas into your head. They have to occur naturally. But, there are ways to keep your mind open to them. That way, you can at least bend those naturally occurring odds in your favor.

First of all...relax. I find ideas are hard to come by if I'm stressed out. Listen to music. Drink your preferred hot beverage. Go to your favorite quiet place (at home or elsewhere). Sit or lay down. Try to reduce distractions as well. Loud noises and busy environments never help ideas to flow. Now, close your eyes, look up at the ceiling, or stare off into nothingness. Do whatever you need to do to clear your mind. Now think. What should you think about? I'll tell you.

The first place I like to mine for ideas is real life. Your own life may not seem interesting to you, but that is simply because you are used to living it. Nearly everyone's life has something about it that could be interesting to others. What is that for you? Maybe you have a unique occupation or hobby. Maybe you've traveled to unique and unusual places. Perhaps you had something in your past that you can't get out of your head. I like to think back on my life as if I'm looking through old photographs. You may see something that catches your eye.

You may have heard the phrase, "Write what you know." This is a good place to start, but I like to say, "Write what you know or want to know." If you have an idea about something in your life that would make a great screenplay, you are in luck. Pick that idea. But, if that's not the case, there are also perfectly viable things that happened to friends and family, your neighbor, or your mailman. Maybe you heard a crazy rumor about a guy down the street, or your friend's mom lived an extraordinary life, or a stranger in a bar told you an insane story, etc. Now, I'm not saying lift people's lives beat-for-beat, but many times, real life can become fiction with a few details changed. Pick different names, combine people's traits, change locations, and add any creative flourishes you want. Mix in as much fiction as you want. Before you know it, you have a handful of characters and events that can be the seeds of a growing screenplay.

NOTE: Basing your screenplay on people you know or stories you've heard is not the same as a screenplay "based on a true story." To write one of those, you need the life rights to a person's story which are more than a little difficult to obtain. And if you go ahead anyway and write an "unauthorized" version of a real person's life, you open yourself up to all sorts of legal action. While a screenplay based on a person's life or events that actually happened may seem like an enticing idea, I highly recommend that you don't write one for your first script.

Another great way to find ideas is to simply be more curious. Be massively curious. Be a sponge. Soak in all the information you can about the world. What subjects interest you? Science? Economics? Technology? Extreme ironing? Everyone has at least one facet of society they are curious about. Pick the thing that you're into and learn as much as you can about it. I can't tell you how many rabbit holes I've been down on the internet simply gathering ideas. If you never stop learning, you'll never run out of ideas. The world we live in is an infinitely interesting and complex place. People, animals, places, languages, oceans, food, politics, music, war, love, death, religion, natural disasters, history…these and many, many more subjects are all fair game for your screenplay. An enormously vast amount of information is available to you about anything. Just pick something you like and hit the internet. While you're searching up your subject, just think, "Would this make a great movie?" Chances are, something will make you say yes.

The simplest way to find ideas for a screenplay is an obvious one. You've already been doing it: consuming media. Our lives today are saturated with art. Movies, TV, books, music, and paintings are more accessible than ever before. The best way to figure out what makes a good movie or screenplay is to simply watch movies and TV. Since most of us have been doing this all of our lives, you've already got an ingrained idea of what is good and bad. The thing that can help you come up with an idea of your own is to think more analytically about what you consume. Rewatch some of your favorite movies and TV shows. Keep a notepad handy and write down the answers to some questions. What makes you like them? What works in the story and why? What makes an impact? What's your favorite scene and why? What would you change or improve? What if you changed the time period? What if the characters had different jobs? Were different genders? Were divorced instead of married? What if that interesting side character was the main character? Also, watch some of the movies and TV you don't like. What doesn't work? Why? If the opposite happened in your script, would it become good? All of these questions can get your creativity stirred up. This is fertile ground for your own ideas.

Moreover, reading books and articles, listening to music, looking at art, or even watching the news can help you come up with ideas. Almost any piece of media contains a story or narrative, whether it is obvious or not. With movies and TV, it is self-evident. But even a still photograph or a painting has a story to it. Pick your favorite photo or painting and look up the history. Often, you'll find stories that can be just as interesting as the art they produced. You just have to be curious.

Another excellent way to get ideas while also familiarizing yourself with screenplays is to read the screenplays of your favorite films. It is getting easier and easier to get your hands on quality, in some cases Academy Award Winning, screenplays. There are myriad ways to get them online. Many are free to download. Want to read the screenplay for your favorite film? Just search the title followed by "screenplay PDF download." More often than not, you can find a copy free of charge. Want a physical copy? eBay is your friend. I've found hard copies of some of my favorite films' scripts for very reasonable prices (under $30). In some cases, the scripts were even used during the production. Other resources are script specific sites like Script City (scriptcity.com) and The Internet Movie Script Database (imsdb.com). Additionally, many famous scripts have been published in book form and are available at bookstores and online. See Appendix B at the back of this book for a list of screenplays (and the films that go with them) that I recommend. My advice is to read as many as you can get your hands on, starting with your favorite films. This is a great way to trigger your imagination for your own movie script. As a huge bonus, you will also familiarize yourself with the format and construction of some of the best scripts in the history of cinema.

The main takeaways here are: be infinitely curious and write down all of your observations. Any time you have even the slightest grain of an idea, write it down. It can be nearly anything in the beginning: a scene idea, a character, a piece of dialogue, a location, a basic concept for a plotline, something funny you overheard, anything. At this stage, don't worry about it fitting into some larger concept. It doesn't even really have to make sense right now. Gathering ideas at the start of your process is the key. Finding where to put them will come later. You need to collect the puzzle pieces before you can figure out how they fit together.

Chapter 4

SHAPING
YOUR IDEA

deas and concepts for your story can (and should) come in many shapes and sizes. Character traits, plot points, locations, subplots, dialogue, and many others can come to you at any time. Once you've gotten them written down, how do you know where in your script they fit? Are they a viable concept for the entire story, or merely a detail? Go over your notes and examine your basic concepts. The two main components you focus on at this point should be characters and story/plot. Without interesting characters and a solid plot, you don't have a screenplay.

Characters

Your characters are the most important part of your screenplay. Once more for the folks in the back:

YOUR CHARACTERS ARE THE MOST IMPORTANT PART OF YOUR SCREENPLAY!

If the audience doesn't care about your characters, they won't care about the movie, plain and simple. How do you make the audience care? Make your characters feel like real people. The more real a character feels, the more relatable they will be. The more relatable they are, the more the audience will care about them. The audience has to feel like they know your characters in the same way they know people in their lives. Think about the characters in one of your favorite films. Why do you like that character? Chances are they are similar, at least in some ways, to you or the people you know in real life. This is the key to any great character in a screenplay.

How do you write a character that the audience feels like they know? You, the writer, have to know them better than anyone. This is where basing them on real people can come in handy. You don't have to base a character entirely on someone you know. A trick I like to use is to compile traits from several different people into one character. Got a stubborn uncle? A caring best friend? A hilarious teacher at school? Add those traits together. If you're observant with people you see and interact with, you'll soon have a host of interesting traits to put together when you're writing. When building a character, using those realistic traits in conjunction with your story will help you build a realistic character. We'll dive even deeper into characters later.

Story

The main question here is: How big of an idea do you have? Does the story have a defined beginning, middle, and end or is it something that feels shorter than that? I can't tell you how many first time writers have come up with a 40 minute movie script. New writers tell me their concept, sometimes a great concept, but it simply doesn't have enough material for a feature film. I often end up saying, "That sounds great. Now, what happens in the last hour of the movie?" They try to write it and give up on page 40 (or earlier) because they run out of story. A film is not a TV show. It doesn't get wrapped up in 21-52 minutes. A feature-length film has many ups and downs, twists and turns, victories and defeats. It has a story that can unfold over time. The main conflict is not quickly or easily solvable. Think of a TV show you like. A sitcom, for instance, is called that for a reason. A "situation comedy" can wrap up its situation in 20-30 minutes. A situation isn't a plot. It's not a story. It's shorter than that.

Example: "A woman is on a train and her ex-boyfriend gets on with his new girlfriend." That is a situation. That can be solved in a short period of time. While it could be an episode of a TV show, it's unlikely to have the narrative heft to sustain a feature film. You need to think bigger. Think expansively. What can sustain a feature is a series of situations that can evolve and change over a longer period of time. Now, let's put that example into a film context.

"A female assassin is on the run after a botched hit. She gets on a train and her ex-boyfriend gets on with his new girlfriend. She realizes that his new girlfriend is her next target. Turns out, the girlfriend is a spy for a foreign government and the boyfriend has no idea." See the difference? The second example has many questions that can be answered over the course of time. Does our protagonist make herself known to her ex-boyfriend? Who or what is she escaping by getting on the train in the first place? If she carries out her next assignment, will the ex-boyfriend get in the way? Will he help her instead? Does she still love him? These are all ways that the story can expand in both directions from the story we have so far. From here, we can formulate a beginning, middle, and end. Or, more to the point, Act One, Act Two, and Act Three. This is the mindset you have to have when testing the strength of your ideas.

The real test of your plot is how it changes over time. You want your characters to go through a lot of transformative events. You want your story to start and end in completely different places; literally, figuratively, or both. You want to take your reader, and by extension, the audience on a journey. The way to do this is to come up with conflict. Conflict is the root of all storytelling. It is exceedingly difficult, if not impossible, to write a film without conflict. You have to put elements at odds with each other and let them combust. Characters who want something but can't have it for whatever reason. That's where the drama lies. You may have heard the term "intention and obstacle." This is a basic concept to keep in mind when coming up with your story. Your story and characters can't change or evolve without your ability to say, "but then this happens" or "because that happened this happens" or "but first this happens." Your story has to have obstacles that are overcome. You have to constantly ask yourself what would prevent your story from going smoothly for your characters. Everything going well for your characters is a quick way to write a boring film. You have to throw up those obstacles. I'll sum this section up with an old screenwriting adage: "How do you write a movie? Take a character, put them up a tree, throw rocks at them, get them out of the tree." It's that simple and that difficult.

Build Your World

A term you'll hear a lot in screenwriting is "world building." This simply means establishing the location of your story and how the world works in that location. Also known as the rules of the world. While this can continue throughout the script, the main bulk of it happens in the first 10 pages. World building is most common in science fiction and fantasy films. This is because they usually take place somewhere very different from our normal world. That's why they must establish where the story takes place and what can and can't happen in that world. Films like *Star Wars* and *Blade Runner* are known for their world building. Those types of worlds have a special set of rules that are different from those we encounter every day. That said, even outside of sci-fi and fantasy, it still helps to think about your location. If your story takes place in a small farming community or a large city, those two stories should be vastly different from each other based on location.

Think about the rules of your world. Can people read minds? Were cars never invented in your world? Perhaps no one can speak or see? The further from reality the concepts in your world are, the sooner you should introduce them. This helps cement the world in your audience's minds and prevents confusion later. If your audience knows early on that people can fly in your world, it won't surprise them when someone does it on page 85. However, if page 85 is the first time someone flies, the audience will be confused, or worse, upset that this rule comes out of nowhere.

The important thing is to establish where your story takes place and how the world functions in that place. Once you set up the rules of your world, stick to them. This will help the audience get absorbed into your story and not get confused or upset later on. At this stage of your idea, devote time to what the world of your screenplay will be. Write down the location and rules of your world in your notes, so that you can refer back to them when fleshing out your first ten pages later.

Set The Reality Bar

Perhaps the most important rule of your world to keep in mind is where the reality bar is set. What this means is simply how realistic the world you are writing about is. Is the reality bar set as low as possible? Then anything can happen no matter how impossible in reality. When the reality bar is set low, there are fantasy creatures, magic spells, fictional planets, other dimensions, etc. Examples include the previously mentioned *Star Wars* and *Blade Runner* as well as *Dark City*, *The Fifth Element*, and more. Alternatively, is your reality bar set very high as in crime films and family dramas? In these films, nothing that can't happen in the real world can happen in your script. No fantasy creatures or magic powers, only what is realistic. Examples include *Good Will Hunting (1997)*, *City of God (2002)*, and *You Can Count On Me (2000)*. Then there are films where the reality is heightened but not completely unrealistic. This often happens in horror or adventure films. The film presents a realistic world but includes unrealistic or fantastical elements. Examples include *Raiders of the Lost Ark*, *Hereditary*, and *Inception*.

The level of reality in your screenplay is not something that should ever be stated outright but should be shown visually in your writing. Don't simply state that the hero is tougher than any real person, have them take a bullet and keep on fighting. Don't tell the reader that we are in another galaxy, have the hero jump in a spaceship and blast off to another planet. However and wherever you choose to set the reality bar in your world, it is important to keep it in mind throughout the writing process. Once set, stick to the level of reality in your script and your world will be consistent and engaging to your audience.

What To Do When You Get Stuck

It's going to happen. You're going to get stuck. There will be a point when you can't make one scene connect with another, you can't move a character from one place to another, you can't figure out what someone will say. If the ideas just aren't coming, don't despair. It happens to every single writer at some point. A term that you shouldn't use is "writer's block." This is a dangerous term. What makes it dangerous is how writers use it as an excuse for not writing. They use it as a reason to give up. A reason not to try. The way they use it is similar to how a person on a diet treats one slip up. They ate a donut so now the whole diet is ruined. Might as well give up on it. Writer's block is the same. They couldn't figure out a scene for a day or two and now they have "writer's block." Might as well give up, right? This is the mindset of someone who won't finish their screenplay. You don't have writer's block, you're just stuck on something. There are ways to get unstuck. These methods can be used throughout the writing process, not just at the start. Here are some that I use:

- **Idea walks:** My favorite way to get the ideas flowing is to simply go on a leisurely stroll. Grab your pocket notepad (or phone notepad) and get out of the house. I also like to make a music playlist to listen to on the walk. I like to put together a mix of music that I would love to hear on the soundtrack of the film my script could eventually become. Most of these playlists consist of music from other films in the genre I'm working in. Lots of musical scores work well for this. If you're writing a film that emulates some of your favorites, put those films' soundtracks on the playlist. Then simply walk around your neighborhood or anywhere you choose. Don't have a specific destination in mind. Allow yourself (and your mind) to relax. Listen to the music, have your notepad ready, and think about your scenes. Get yourself in a calm, open headspace. Picture your movie in your head. What comes next? Let the ideas come naturally. When you have an idea, get it down in your notes. Even a single line of an idea can break open your whole story. Aside from getting ideas, this also helps to get you away from your script for a bit. A blank page staring back at you can be intimidating. That can scare your ideas away. Go on a walk. Allow yourself to unwind a bit from your writing session. The ideas will come.

- **Talk it out:** This might seem obvious, but you'd be surprised how many screenwriters don't actually read their script out loud. Ideally, actors will be saying these lines in a film, so saying them aloud is almost like the first time your movie exists anywhere other than the page. At a certain point, you need to hear what you are writing. Many times, that point is when you get stuck. Ask yourself, "Does this sound natural?" "Is this getting across the information I want?" "Does this make sense?" "Does it flow?" Often, simply saying a piece of dialogue or description aloud will expose its weak points. After fixing weak points, you can now ask yourself, "What comes next?"

- **Talk to others:** Tell people about your story. I have countless times that I've been stuck on a certain part of my script and simply explaining it to someone else breaks me free. Friends, family, coworkers, whoever. I've had times when I was explaining my script to someone and thought of a way to fix it while I was talking. They had no idea that I fixed my problem out loud on the spot. I immediately got those ideas down and implemented them during my next writing session. Also, I've had someone suggest the tiniest change to my story and it completely corrected my problem. Now, I'm not saying you should blab on and on to those who aren't interested. Ask if they want to hear your story first. Simply telling your story to someone, especially non-writers, can be an unexpectedly huge help if you're stuck in a writing rut.

- **Do more research:** As a writer, information is your best friend. You should constantly be learning new information regarding your script's topics. Many times you will get hung up on plot points. How do these two characters meet? If this door is locked, how does the hero get it open? How does the group of friends get from the house to the fairgrounds? Researching the topics that are holding up your story can break down those barriers. Technical information can be especially helpful. That door the hero needs to get through might have a weak brand of lock they can break. Not sure what type? Research. Character in a shootout, but not sure what gun they have? Research. The character's car keeps breaking down but you're not sure what make and model would be prone to that? Research. Gaining knowledge of the topics, people, events, and tools within your story can lead to new paths for it to take.

- **Add more character obstacles:** Sometimes you can get stuck because you can't think of what your characters should do next. This is because they have it too easy. Things always working out well is what leaves characters stagnating. If they have a harder time with more obstacles, they have more to overcome. More to overcome means more action to take, which means more plot. More plot means your script will start moving again.

- **Break out of the box:** Having a well thought out plan of what your story should be is a good thing. But sometimes, you can get stuck on what you thought the script should be *before* you write it and not allow it to become something else *as* you write it. Don't get too stuck on what your original plan for a scene or character should be. It's essential to have an idea or plan but be aware that you might have to change it if the story dictates that. Your screenplay is constantly evolving. Let it happen. If you hold too tightly to your initial ideas, that can prevent new ideas from flowing. Sometimes, you have to let go of an old idea to let new ones in.

- **Move on:** It's easy to get hung up on a scene or sequence that isn't working. But the truth is, there is likely another scene that you will have no problems with. While I am an advocate of writing from start to finish, that is not always possible. If it helps you get unstuck, then I suggest simply jumping to another scene that you have a clear idea for. Write that scene and come back. It's like taking a math test where you run into a problem you can't solve. Do you simply fail the test? No. You move on to the problems you can tackle, then come back around. By the time you've written another scene or two, you can come back to the problem scene with a fresh perspective. If you're lucky, the finished later scenes can fix the problems you were struggling with in earlier scenes. It's important to remember that just because one scene isn't working right now, doesn't mean another scene elsewhere won't.

- **Shake it up:** Flipping a scene around can also be helpful. If a scene feels lifeless, ask yourself if the opposite of the scene's original intent would work better. If a character gives an impassioned speech at the end of a scene, what if they started the scene with it? What if a character died in a car crash instead of surviving? What if the couple stayed together instead of breaking up? Sometimes, the opposite of what was planned can spin your story in another more interesting direction. Don't be afraid to flip your scenes' outcomes, intent, or emphasis. Another thing to do is shuffle the order of the scenes themselves. If a major character dies earlier, lovers reunite later or the end scene becomes the first scene, this can change the entire dynamic of the script and can open up all sorts of possibilities for improvement. Don't close yourself off to major changes. Be open to shake ups. You never know what will fall out.

| Chapter 5 |

IDEA SUMMARY

Alright, you've got a handful of notes you feel good about. There's a general plot in your mind and you have a character or two to go with it. This is great! You're right where you need to be in the process. So what do you do now with this smattering of scribbles? Remember those yellow notepads? Grab one.

Now you're going to consolidate your notes in this one notepad. I start with a summary of my general idea in as few sentences as possible. Then I cut it down to one sentence. The industry term for this is a "logline." This is simply the shortest possible explanation of your concept. They are one sentence that has under 50 words. Here are a few famous examples:

- *"The aging patriarch of an organized crime dynasty transfers control of his clandestine empire to his reluctant son." (The Godfather, 1972)*

- *"A 17-year-old high school student is accidentally sent thirty years into the past in a time-traveling DeLorean invented by his close friend, a maverick scientist." (Back to the Future, 1985)*

- *"A computer hacker learns from mysterious rebels about the true nature of his reality and his role in the war against its controllers." (The Matrix, 1999)*

See how simple and effective those are? Loglines are an art form unto themselves and I don't expect you to craft a perfect one right out of the gate. I often refine and polish mine after the screenplay is written. That said, it is a great idea to write a basic logline for your script as soon as you feel you have a grasp on your idea. This will help solidify it in your mind and will help when others inevitably ask, "What is your movie about?" Write your logline at the top of the first page of your notepad. It serves as excellent motivation.

After that, the best thing to do is just get it all out. Every single idea you've written down, copy it over into this notebook. It's incredibly important at this stage to not judge your ideas. Never evaluate your scribbles before putting them into the idea summary. Many times, ideas can seem like they won't fit into the story or are just plain bad.

But, those very same ideas can fit in perfectly once the rough draft is being written. You never know.

The important thing right now is to simply get the ideas out and collected into one cohesive document. This stage is about funneling your notes into something more manageable. With that in mind, this notepad is where some real organization can happen. After writing the aforementioned logline at the top, I organize my main idea notepad as follows:

Storyline/Plot: A short summary of the story from beginning to end. You don't need a fully fleshed out, moment-by-moment story at this point. Just get down what you have. At the very least, get an idea of the beginning, middle, and end. Label them as such. If you don't have this all worked out yet, that's okay. But, now is when you'll need to focus your thinking in that direction.

Scenes: Chances are, by this point, you'll have at least a few specific scenes in mind. Writing a romance? You'll probably need a way for your characters to meet for the first time. Maybe you even have an idea for how they break up or get back together. Great! Get all of it down, no matter how insignificant the details seem now. Have a great idea for a chase scene in your post-apocalyptic thriller? Perfect! Put it down on paper. You get the picture. Simple and short summaries will do for now.

Characters: By now you should have a decent idea of the main character aka the protagonist. If not, now's a great time to start. I put them down with a brief summary of who they are. This can include anything you have from quirks and personality to the clothes they wear to the job they have. Any details you have will help. Do the same with any other characters you have, starting with villains and working down to the smaller supporting characters. This will also help you to start thinking about what characters your story needs to flow and make sense. In addition, you can start to think of the types of people they are, which makes them more real in your mind.

Questions: Here's where you can suss out what is needed. Put down any missing pieces you have. Any part of the story that is missing, character motivations, logistics, etc. should go in this section. If you're anything like me, you'll have a lot. That's okay. Don't get discouraged if your story has plot holes at this stage. Another open secret: every story has plot holes (until they're filled). Not sure how your main character survives a plane crash? Good. Write down, "How do they survive the plane crash?" If you have ideas about scenes, start thinking about how to get from one to the other. Write down your concerns and questions, no matter how seemingly small and insignificant. Do the same with your characters. If your protagonist needs to hate snakes for the story to work, why they hate snakes will need answering, etc. Getting every possible question that needs answering down on paper will help you to think more critically about your story as it develops.

Theme: Try to establish your theme at this stage. Your theme is basically what your story is all about. It can be an overarching idea, an underlying message, moral statement, or central topic. Some examples would be: "self-acceptance," "money doesn't always bring happiness," or "war is hell." Your theme is, in a few words, what your story is about. Not what the plot is. Plot is the series of events of your story. This is where it differs from your logline. Your logline is a short summary of the plot. Your theme is what is at the heart of your story. Theme is what your story is *really* about. See the difference? It's subtle but very important.

Using a large notepad is how you shape your notes into something connected. It is where you can take a series of rambling thoughts and put them down into something resembling a narrative. Don't be afraid to add to your idea as you're writing out this notebook. Any expansion of the idea at this stage is a good thing. Additionally, once you have this notepad, you don't have to refer to many different sources for your notes. At this stage, you can incorporate your smaller notes into this document. Moreover, now you have a fuller version of your idea out of your head in a hard copy. Nothing to forget now.

Clichés to Avoid

Let's look at some overused, unoriginal, and inappropriate elements you shouldn't put in your script. These tend to show up in screenplays from first time writers. This is also not even close to a complete list:

- **It was all a dream:** This is one of the laziest ways to write. It's a cop out. If it turns out that your story was the dream of a character who wakes up at the end, you've just invalidated the audience's experience. You've just robbed them of any authenticity they felt during the experience. The story didn't actually happen. If it didn't actually happen, then why did you just make an audience sit through it? Why did you even write it? This might have been okay 75 years ago, but it's not acceptable today. Don't do it.

- **Heavy-handed social message:** Writing is one of the best ways to criticize those in power, point out injustice, expose a problem, deconstruct a system, or simply bring ideas to the attention of others. There is nothing inherently wrong with this. In fact, if done well, writing can bring about actual social change. The problem arises when you forget to also tell a good story. A screenplay (and film) delivering a message the writer wants to get across has to be handled delicately. The real trick is to be subtle. Social messages and statements don't need to be at the forefront of your narrative to be effective. I would argue that they are more effective when they are stealthily delivered without the audience or reader even realizing it until the film is over. When this is done poorly, the message is the only thing the audience is getting. The characters are simply vessels to deliver the statements the writer wants to make. There is a lack of actual entertainment value in the screenplay. There is no reason to care. There is no reason to keep watching the film or reading the script once the message has been received by the audience. By all means, if you have a statement to make about the world you live in, include it in your screenplay. Just don't forget to include a story worth telling while you do it.

- **An alarm clock wakes up the main character in the first scene:** Your day starts this way, so why shouldn't your character's day start the same way, right? Wrong! This is the easiest and most trite way to start any story. Not just in films. Please, never, ever do this.

- **Overused dialogue:** These are lines you've heard over and over in movies. Many times these are in action films. Examples include: "This is not what I signed up for," "What are you gonna do, shoot me?" "We aren't so different, you and I," "We've got company," "Don't you die on me," "You just don't get it, do you?" etc. The list goes on and on. It's simple: if you've heard the line in more than one movie, don't put it in yours.

- **Using controversial subjects to emotionally manipulate:** Taking on a serious subject matter in a screenplay is not impossible, but it must be done with an extreme amount of care. These subjects include but are not limited to abortion, The Holocaust, 9/11, religion, gun control, racism, and terminal diseases (HIV/AIDS, cancer, etc.). These are subjects that require an enormous amount of respect and caution in their depiction. If handled incorrectly, they can come off as insensitive or even offensive. The worst way to use these subjects is for shock value or to manipulate your audience into unearned emotions. These are real life issues that happen to real people. They are not there to be used as a plot device or prop for someone who isn't skilled enough to earn emotional responses from their writing. The only real exception to this is if you have a personal connection to the topic you are covering. For example, you are writing about your personal battle with cancer. Another would be if you are writing a Holocaust drama based on the stories of your grandparent who lived through it. If you don't have a personal connection to or reason for writing about a hot-button issue, don't do it.

- **"Enhance":** We've all seen this one. An investigator of some kind makes a photograph larger or "enhanced" to spot some minute clue. This has appeared countless times, from great films like *Blade Runner* to every terrible TV cop show. One of the earliest examples is in *Call Northside 777*. That film came out in 1948. That was almost 75 years ago. This trope has seen its day and then some. It's over. It's dead. Don't use it.

- **Pop culture references:** We all have our favorite movies, music, books, and people. It can be tempting to honor those things in your film by name dropping them. Others probably like those things too, so why not make your script more relatable by mentioning them, right? Wrong. All this does is make people think about those other movies that you just mentioned, taking them out of your story. Also, why instantly compare your work to someone else's that is more successful? That's a bad idea. Another reason not to do this is that it isn't needed. You don't need to name your influences when writing. They will come out naturally. There has been times when someone has told me a scene I'd written reminded them of a film or book that had influenced me and I didn't even realize I was paying tribute to it. You don't need to call any more attention to what you like. The audience will get it.

- **Deus Ex Machina:** For those unfamiliar, this term comes from the theater. It refers to an actor, playing God, being lowered down on a platform to magically fix all the problems for the characters. This explains why its literal translation is "God from the machine." These days, it means any plot point that seems to come out of nowhere, no matter how unrealistic, to fix a problem. This usually means that the protagonist is saved at the last moment by something that is not the result of their own actions. Famous examples include: the eagles saving Sam and Frodo in *The Lord of the Rings*, the aliens dying from bacteria in *War of the Worlds*, and the T-rex saving the heroes from the raptors in *Jurassic Park*. It robs the audience of the satisfaction of seeing the hero win on their own merits. It invalidates the hero's actions up to this point. Why should they try if they will just be rescued from outside forces in the end anyway? Don't use this method. Make your characters earn their victories.

- **Love interests who hate each other at first:** Another one that's been done to death. Audiences today are smarter than they get credit for. As soon as two people in a romantic film don't like each other, we know they'll be in love by the end. It's not clever. It's not smart. It's predictable. It's lazy writing.

- **Magic to fix the plot:** If your film has magic in it, don't let it become a crutch to fix plot problems you can't solve logically. I'm sure you've seen a film where there is some sort of threat to the hero and then all of a sudden there is some previously unseen spell that a wizard/superhero/supernatural being can cast to patch that plot hole. It's easy to do and robs the audience of any kind of suspense. If the wizard can cast a spell to fix anything that happens, then why should we care if anything happens to the hero? All of the threat, and therefore suspense or stakes, is gone. Have all the magic and wizards you want, just don't make them story fixing wizards.

Chapter 6

SCENE CARDS

Remember those 3 x 5 index cards? Time to break them out. Using them as scene cards is an invaluable step in the process. Without having to think too much about them, you can quickly get down scene ideas. The great thing about that is you don't have to know where the scene fits into the story right away. Simply put down any scene you think might work in your script in a few words. You can decide whether it does or not later. Scene cards let you produce ideas as fast as you can think of them without any filter or editing. As soon as your mind is working on your screenplay, start writing out any scenes that come to you. Traditionally, when writing scene cards, it's best to keep things brief. Mine tends to be three to five words, like "gunfight," "protagonist discovers secret," or "escape." But, this is not a set in stone rule. Be descriptive as you wish. The main thing is to get your scene ideas out when you think of them, even if they don't fit into your script as it exists in its current state.

Another major reason I use scene cards is you can lay them out in rows and see how your story is flowing. Once you have a stack of them (I end up with 40 to 50 depending on the script length) lay them out on a large flat surface (kitchen table, bed, etc.) in order from start to finish. Some writers use sticky notes and put them up on the wall. The choice is yours. This is beneficial because it's the first time you can "see" your screenplay from beginning to end. Once you have the cards laid out, you will be able to see what parts of your story are still missing and need filling in. Some parts you'll know right away, like if you don't know your ending yet. That's okay. Just lay out what cards you have so you can pinpoint your story's deficiencies. Trust me, at this stage, you'll have some. Again, don't worry. This is why we make scene cards. Now, once you've put them down, what I like to do is picture the movie in my head as I read the cards, sometimes out loud. What this does is allows you to see how your scenes flow together. For example, let's say your protagonist learns a piece of crucial information and you have scene cards written where they already know that information and scenes where they don't yet know it placed together, that's something to work on. Now you can see that you need to add the scene or scenes where they learn that information. Then you can stick a card in between that says something like "protagonist learns crucial information." This also forces you to think about what I like to call "connecting scenes." These are small scenes that move the story along logically to get the audience from one point to another. For example, let's say I have a scene card that says, "bank robbery," and I have another later in the story that says, "gang questions protagonist about money." Now I know I need a connecting scene or scenes in between those two larger scenes. So, continuing the example, now I write out "protagonist stashes money" and "gang kidnaps protagonist" and I put those cards in between my larger scenes. Instead of two disconnected large scenes, I have four scenes that flow together. See how that works?

Another valuable thing about writing and laying out your scene cards is it allows you to add and subtract scenes freely. I often remove cards once I realize I've already conveyed that information earlier or later in the script. Tip: don't throw out any scene cards until the script is finished. You never know when a scene you previously thought wasn't needed can fit in later. I keep a stack of "cut" scene cards in the back of my main stack. Also, if you're not sure if a scene is needed, flip the card sideways and skip over it when reading through the cards. If you feel like you can cut that scene, stick the card in the "cut" pile. If not, flip it back and keep it in.

Reordering and rearranging scene cards is also a good reason to lay them all out. This way, you can reshuffle at what point a scene happens in the story. Sometimes, you are positive a scene is in the right place until you see the scenes that are before and after it. Perhaps the big reveal you were sure has to take place in the last twenty pages will work better in the middle of the story. Maybe the villain sees the error of his or her ways ten scenes earlier. Don't be afraid to move your scene cards around in drastic ways to shake up your story. I've even taken a photo of one card layout (to preserve my first idea) and then completely rearranged the whole plot just to see what interesting things happen. Does that always work? No. Will you always learn something about your story? Yes.

Sometimes, scene ideas can feel similar but have a few key differences. For example, let's say you know you need a scene where a married couple argues. In one version they argue over money, but it might also work if they argue over their kids' needs. What I like to do is write the stronger of the two on the front of the card with an arrow pointing to the alternate version written on the back. This allows you to have the alternate version just in case you find out later that it works better. With the amount most screenplays change throughout writing, it's always a good idea to hedge your bets with solutions. You can never have enough ideas and you never know when an alternate idea will end up working perfectly later on.

If you wish to push the scene card idea even further, you can purchase colored index cards. Then you can assign each character or plot line a specific color. With this technique, you can have a visual representation of each element of the script. When laid out, you can quickly tell which characters and plots are dominating your script and what others need more attention or development.

It is incredibly helpful to see your story as one long, flowing, progressive body rather than a choppy collection of scenes. Writing scene cards and laying them out will give you a complete picture of your script without having to flip through pages of notes. Having this overview of the building blocks of the script will allow you to fill in gaps and shore up any issues you may have at this stage of your writing. Remember, this stage is about getting a picture in your mind about how your story and screenplay unfold. Lay out your scene cards and read them through as many times as you feel is needed. It's something that you can't do too often. I write scene cards up until I have a rough draft of the screenplay. They are the quickest and easiest way to get your ideas out quickly and fit them into the story easily.

Chapter 7

TIMELINE(S)

G rab the notepad with your general idea summary on it. Grab your scene cards as well. In the notepad, flip past the summary by a few pages. Now you'll group events into a timeline. This is another way of visualizing your story, and as such, some writers like to put this on a larger canvas. I know folks who use a whiteboard with markers, an artist's sketch pad, chalkboards, etc. If you're a visual learner and want to use something bigger, go for it. I like to use the same notepad to keep everything in one place. The fewer implements to keep track of, the better.

Making a timeline is fairly simple. All you have to do is write out clusters of events in the order they happen. Start at the beginning of your story and write short summaries of the main events in the story. Don't use complete sentences. Don't put in any dialogue. What you want are little word clusters. Each cluster should have two to three main events that take place in the story. Make sure the events are written in chronological order. Using your scene cards here is essential. What is important here is that these are not individual scenes, they are groups of events.

Now that you have a cluster of events, simply draw an arrow to the next cluster of events. Write out the next few things that happen. Repeat this process until you reach the end of the story. If you have names for your characters, put them in. If not, just use "protagonist" (for brevity I use "protag"), and "antagonist" (antag). If you don't have names yet for your supporting characters, you can simply designate them how you wish. "Mom," "Cop," "Bartender," "Best Friend," and the like are perfectly acceptable at this point. A timeline usually is three to five pages long. Once you have your timeline completed, read it through. If you have a section of your timeline that feels slow or lacking in scenes, that's when you can write out some more scene cards for that part of the script. If you're missing a key part in your story right now, such as the ending, now is a good time to think of something. But, if you can't come up with something you're happy with, put in a placeholder. Sometimes, I'll even just write "Finale" as my final word cluster. What's important is that you group your scene ideas into a series of events. And that you slot in the characters that are partaking in those events. This is how you get an understanding of how your story moves in time from start to finish.

Once you have a timeline that feels cohesive, now is when you need to think about pacing. Remember in your General Idea Summary how it helps to think about a beginning, middle, and end? Now is the time to lock that in with Acts 1, 2, and 3. Within your timeline, put in where those act breaks are going to be. I like to write in "End Act 1" and so on, after a word cluster that ends an act. Here's a simple breakdown of the three act structure to help:

Act 1: Introduce your characters and your world. Toward the end of the act, plant the seeds for the conflict in Act 2. (aka "Put someone up a tree.")

Act 2: Introduce your conflict. Make your protagonist struggle against it. Toward the end of the act, set up possible solutions to the conflict. (aka "Throw rocks at them.")

Act 3: Resolve the conflict. Your protagonist overcomes the obstacles or succumbs to them. (aka "Get them out of the tree.")

Deciding on your act breaks depends on the momentum or rhythm of your scenes. Or, in this case, the clusters of events. Act 1 should end at a slower speed or level of excitement than it starts. For example, if your first act started with an action sequence, the end of the act could be a dialogue scene. Now, the start of Act 2 can begin with something faster. Since the first act ended with dialogue, now the second act can begin with an exciting sequence. The same can be repeated for Act 3, slowing down at the conclusion of the story.

The rhythm of the sequences is vitally important to keep the reader interested. With that in mind, take a look at your timeline and break up the action so the pacing is changing regularly. If your story starts with an hour of dialogue and ends with 40 minutes of non-stop action, your reader (and audience) is going to feel bored at first and exhausted at the end. That is not how you want your story to play out. What works better is if there is a variable level of excitement throughout. For example, let's say you have four scenes total: two dialogue scenes and two action scenes. They will read better if you alternate the scenes. Action-dialogue-action-dialogue will be better than action-action-dialogue-dialogue. It's best to switch up your pacing. This can be achieved by revealing information that changes the direction of the story. This is often referred to as "a reversal."

The use of reversals can help you plot out your timeline. When grouping your sequence clusters, think in terms of reversals. Did you just finish up a scene with a load of dialogue? Reverse the next scene with some physical action. Just finished a car chase? Reverse the next scene with some dialogue back at the hideout. You get the picture. I try to have a reversal every 10 pages or so of my script. This is not a completely strict page count, but it's good to keep in mind while writing. It especially helps to keep your pace moving along. If you notice you've had action scenes for 15 pages straight, that's when you know you should break up that action with some downtime.

A word of warning about reversals: don't overuse them. The pace changing up every 10 pages or so is fine. Every two pages? Now you've got a problem. You don't want your reader, and by extension, your audience, getting whiplash trying to keep track of the ever-changing pace of your movie. Just use your best judgment and instincts here. A good exercise is to watch two of your favorite movies. One that is fast paced, like an action movie. And one that is slower, like a character driven drama. Keep track of the reversals in each, either in your head or with a notepad. This will teach you an enormous amount about pacing. Now, think about your timeline and what your goals are. Are you writing an action movie full of excitement, or a drama full of emotion? The use of reversals and tempo changes can help you plan out your timeline so the pacing of your script keeps your reader engaged throughout.

Chapter 8

CHARACTER DEVELOPMENT

've said it before, but it bears repeating…your characters are the most important part of your script. You need to know them inside and out. As if they are your own family and friends. So how do you do this? As noted previously, basing them on real people or an amalgam of real people is a good place to start. But after that, you need to dig into their history as a person. You need to flesh them out. You need to make them feel real.

First of all, use the character history form in Appendix A at the back of this book. It will help you sort out practically every aspect of your character. I have formulated those questions over many years and many screenplays. I use it for every major character in every screenplay I write. It is long and exhaustive. It may seem like it is overkill. This is on purpose. You can never know too much about your characters. There may be questions in there that you feel you don't need to know. I understand. But think of it this way: your character should feel like a real person that you know, therefore, you should know some things that you wish you didn't. Knowing your characters' vulnerabilities, insecurities, and internal obstacles will make them better. Knowing your characters intimately, sometimes embarrassingly so, will help your audience relate to them. Intimate details in a character that an audience can relate to are extremely impactful.

To be honest with you, character histories are my least favorite part of prepping a screenplay. It can become tedious at times. That being said, there has never been a single time while writing my rough draft that it didn't help. Fill out a history for each of your major characters that affect the story. For example, if your script is about a love triangle, you immediately know that you'll be filling out at least three histories. In other words, you should fill out a history for your protagonist, villain, and supporting characters. You don't need to fill one out for a waiter that serves food in one scene.

Let's take a basic look at the types of characters you can put in your script. Keep these in mind when filling out your character histories, and when fleshing out your plot.

Protagonist/Hero/Main Character

The character who will be the main focus of the story and go on the main journey of the screenplay. This character will most likely appear throughout the entire script. And, in some cases, the protagonist is in every single scene.

You may have heard that you absolutely must make your protagonist likable. This is true, but only to a degree. "Likable" or "likability" are words you will hear many times about your characters throughout your writing career. For your first screenplay, it's a good idea to make your protagonist quite likable. Don't be alarmed if your character doesn't necessarily fit that description. The nice part about this term is it is fairly subjective. What makes a character likable? Is it only characters who are morally pure according to societal standards? Is it someone who does bad things, but is charming? What about someone who is morally flawed but redeems themselves over the course of the story? The answer is, if done right, it can be any or all of these. It's your story, so if you want to write about a firefighter who rescues cats from trees or a serial killer who goes on a rampage, there are ways to make them likable. Most audiences *want* to like your main character, so all you have to do is give them something to like. It can be a facet of their personality, the actions they take, or the goal they are seeking.

The other aspect of a successful main character is motivation. They have to want something. And there has to be something in their way. No one wants to read a script where the main character is inactive and passive. It will feel flat and fake if your character doesn't care about anything. Your character needs to have a central desire that they want to achieve more than anything in the world. It can be as simple as a hamburger or as complex as world peace, but they have to *need* it. If you think about most beloved movie characters, it is quite easy to point out what they want. This is important: keep what they want simple. How they get there can be complex, but the goal should be easy to summarize.

Let's look at some famous examples:

- Luke Skywalker (*Star Wars, 1977*): He needs to save the galaxy from destruction by Darth Vader and his empire.

- Elizabeth Bennett (*Pride & Prejudice, 2005*): She wants to marry someone she actually loves, not just someone who is rich.

- Marty McFly (*Back to the Future, 1985*): He has to get his parents together in the past so he'll exist again in the future.

These characters are noteworthy because they are motivated. And those motives are simply stated. I wrote those summaries from memory. That's how enduring those characters are. A motivated main character is an interesting character. Your reader and audiences want to go on a journey and your main character is their guide. Journeys don't begin with laziness and lack of desire, they come from motivation and goals. As a bonus, a strong motivation will also enhance your character's likability. We humans are hardwired to like and respect anyone who has goals and is willing to strive to achieve them. The doers. The go-getters. People of action are what other people are interested in.

A highly motivated, likable protagonist does not mean flawless. Making a character relatable means making them feel like a realistic person. That means, they should have imperfections, vulnerabilities, and concerns. No real person is without flaws, therefore, your protagonist should have them as well. Maybe they are a people pleaser. Maybe they are insecure. Perhaps they are cold and unfeeling. There is an endless amount of flaws and foibles that your characters can have. Make sure to give them at least one major one. I like to give them an event in their past that they don't like to talk about or think about. This lends an air of mystery to the character and gives me something to reveal to the audience later at any time for maximum impact. The main thing is that you use flaws and emotional wounds to make your character feel more real. Make sure they aren't perfect. As much as we'd like to be, no one is perfect. That means perfect characters are not relatable and should be avoided.

Antagonist/Villain

This character is your hero's main opposition. They are the one standing in the way of your protagonist's goal. They are the obstacle. In many ways, they are the exact opposite of your hero. Throughout the screenplay, the antagonist should be actively working to make sure the protagonist does not achieve their goals. The villain wants the hero to fail.

An interesting facet of villains is that they sometimes are not even a person or physical entity. In some cases, the antagonist of a screenplay can be a concept or the state of the world. Take our previous example of *Pride and Prejudice*. There is no physical villain in that story. The antagonist is the economic structure of arranged marriages. In social justice dramas, the antagonist is the way the world works in the depicted time period. The villain is The System. In many cases, there is a physical person who embodies these ideas or concepts, but this isn't always required. I can't whole-heartedly recommend that you make your villain a concept or system for your very first screenplay, as it can be more complex than a physical being. But, don't let me stop you. If you have an idea for a great social justice drama, by all means, push on.

The main thing to keep in mind when developing your villain (aka antagonist) is that they don't think they are the villain. Every villain thinks they are the hero. They view the hero as the enemy. This is why it is a good idea to humanize your villain in at least a small way. If your villain is a human person, I recommend you treat them just as you would the hero when developing them. Make them feel real. Give them flaws and quirks. What is a villain if not a person whose flaws are too great to overcome? They also should have their own set of intentions and obstacles. And much like your protagonist, they need to be motivated. It's a good idea to make them have at least one understandable motivation. The best villains are ones the audience doesn't necessarily like, but the ones that they can *understand*.

In many ways, the villain is the opposite of the hero. But a better villain is not just the opposite, but a reflection of the hero. Remember those flaws your hero has? The villain knows how to use them against the hero. They are strong in all the ways the hero is weak. And the hero is strong in all the ways the villain is weak. The villain has to be the perfect person to exploit the hero's flaws. And the hero uses the conflict with the villain to overcome those flaws. But, without the villain, this would never have happened. The villain forces the hero to change to achieve their goals. This is what makes them great enemies. They are the mirror image of each other. They actually share some traits. They have simply utilized those traits in different ways. In many cases, the hero could have become the villain had their fate been slightly different and vice-versa.

Let's look at a classic example: Batman vs. The Joker. This is the quintessential hero and villain matchup. They are the perfect reflection of each other. Batman is a genius and is morally pure. The Joker is also a genius but is morally bankrupt. Batman is logical, The Joker is chaotic. Batman will not kill. The Joker is a murderer. Batman upholds the law. The Joker is a criminal. They both know each other's strengths and weaknesses and can use them against the other. This is why they are so perfectly matched. This is why The Joker is used so often in Batman films and why their battle has raged on for decades. It's also not inconceivable that given the right circumstances, The Joker could have become Batman, and vice-versa. They aren't just opposites. They are counterparts.

Supporting/Secondary Characters

These are any characters that still affect the story, but are not the main focus. Some examples include a spouse or partner of the lead character or villain, family members, best friends, wise mentor, the town sheriff, etc. Some characters can have a profound effect on the story or main characters whether they appear throughout the screenplay or in only one scene.

One thing to be sure of when writing a supporting character is to make sure they feel like they belong in the script outside of the plot. What I mean by this is don't make a character that is nothing but a plot device. You don't want a character that is there solely to push the plot forward when it needs to be pushed. For example, if you know your main character needs to haul a bunch of stuff at one point, don't put in a neighbor character that just so happens to own a pickup truck. If that character appears earlier in the script, is well rounded, and has something non-truck related to do as well, then you're on the right track. In other words, don't make up a supporting character to patch holes in your plot.

Giving a supporting character their own mini-story is known as a subplot. These are devices used to round out your supporting characters, tie into the main plot, and/or contrast against or emphasize your main plot's intentions. For example, perhaps your main character is a broken down football star. A supporting character could be his son who doesn't enjoy sports at all and is desperately trying to get into a good college to prove his worth to his father. This subplot fleshes out the son's character while also providing a contrasting point of view the main character must contend with. This is how a subplot can add value to your character while also providing a plot point that doesn't feel contrived.

Use these characters in your script in any way you want, just make sure they are well rounded. Also, don't create side characters to fix plot holes. Each character in your script has their own set of intentions, obstacles, strengths, and flaws, even if they're not expressly stated or explored in the finished script. Remember, supporting characters are there to support the main characters *and* the plot.

Multiple Narratives/Ensemble

An ensemble screenplay is one where there are multiple main characters who each receive an equal amount of screen time. When there are two main characters, it is often called a tandem narrative or "two-hander." Common with multiple narratives, each narrative, usually three or more, is part of a larger story or community within the story. This includes films where large casts of characters are all tied together by a single event. Often, the story will show the event in question from multiple characters' viewpoints, thereby granting the audience a multitude of perspectives.

One good aspect of a multiple narrative screenplay is that it does keep the reader and audience guessing as to what will happen next. With many characters, each one can push the narrative in their own unique way that is new to the audience each time. That being said, I do not recommend that you write a multiple narrative screenplay for your first one.

Reason number one is very simple: it's a lot more work. Coming up with one good plot line can be very challenging enough. Now think of trying to come up with three, or five…or ten. See where I'm going with this? If you have to develop characters that feel real and relatable, that takes time. Quite simply, the more characters, the more time you have to spend fleshing them out. It's best to keep the first screenplay you write simple. One plot line with one main character is plenty for now.

The second reason is balance. Often times, even highly skilled, veteran screenwriters have trouble balancing character with story. It can be a tricky question of how many of those finite script pages you devote to fleshing out characters vs. pushing the narrative forward. Ask yourself this question: how many ensemble films have you seen where at least one or two of the characters or storylines felt underdeveloped? There are plenty of them. Inevitably, the writer is unable to devote enough page space (and, therefore, screen time) to make each plot worth including.

The third and final reason to not write a multiple narrative is the difficulty in tying it all together. Connecting each character and plot line to the overarching story can be extremely challenging. The ending of this kind of script becomes more difficult because you no longer have to wrap up a single story in a satisfying way, you now have to wrap up a variety of stories. That only compounds the amount that the ending has to pay off. In other words, your ending has to now be five times more amazing when you have five stories.

Once again, I must say that I can't stop you. If you still want to write your first script with 25 plots, go for it. If you are positive that you have the perfect way to pull it off, that's great. Don't say I didn't warn you. For now, my advice is to keep things simple. A few characters that the audience cares deeply about are better than ten that they can't remember. Write that dream ensemble script for your second screenplay. Or your sixth.

One last important part about characters: they need names. Ask any screenwriter and they'll tell you that naming characters can be one of the difficult parts of writing. Rarely, you will find the perfect name for a character early on. If you do, savor the moment. You feel like you instantly know a character when you come up with a perfect name. You can even begin to shape the character's personality and traits around the perfect name. Unfortunately, it often is the opposite of this scenario. You'll do all the hard work of fleshing out every last tiny detail of the character only to realize they are still called "Protagonist" or "Main Character" in your notes.

The way to come up with a name for your character is to balance two things. One, how realistic do you want the name to be? This can be according to the character's place of birth, cultural or ethnic heritage, occupation, etc. In other words, how much will the name "match" the character? If your character is a tow truck driver in present day New Jersey, their name being Tony wouldn't seem out of place. However, if they are a Sumerian from ancient Mesopotamia, maybe don't name them Tony. The name should fit the character if you are aiming for realism.

The second factor in choosing a name is how much you want it to tie into the screenplay's themes or messages. If your main character is a police officer, naming them Copman is a bad idea. But, perhaps you want to name them Linton, as in lint, to denote "fuzz" the slang term for the police. Using a name that is related to the plot or subtlety denotes the character's personality is a way to add another layer of meaning to the name. If done poorly, you can come off as pretentious, but it can be done well with enough finesse.

The main reason you want to give thought to the names of your characters is, otherwise, you'll end up with too many common, simple, meaningless names. No one wants to read a script or watch a film where everyone is named Bob, Tim, Mary, and Kim. There is nothing wrong with those names, but your characters will be more complex and layered if they have a name that is related to the story, geography, or symbolism. A good resource I like to use (at the time of writing this book) is the website: behindthename.com. That site is a wealth of information on name meanings and origins. It is a good starting point when you are struggling to name a character and you want the name to have meaning.

Character Arc

This refers to how a character changes over the course of the story. This is a transformation of the character from one type of person at the start of the screenplay to another type of person at the end of the screenplay.

The factors that drive the character arc are what the character wants and what the character needs. What the character wants is known to the character. It is usually something external (for example: a new bike). It also is something that may not grant the character the happiness or peace they desire if they attain it. It is what drives the character to attain their goals. What the character needs is unknown to the character (example: appreciation for loved ones). This is what will grant the character the happiness or peace they didn't know they needed once attained. This internal, unspoken need is what is really driving the character on their journey.

When it comes to your character's arc, you get to decide if they achieve their external or internal goals. If they get what they want, need, both, or neither. How your character changes over the story is totally up to you. Whatever you decide, just make sure you, as the screenwriter, are happy with the result at the end. If you want your character to get everything they want and it makes them a better person in the end, do it. Conversely, you can deny the character any of their wants and needs and they become a husk of a person at the end of the story. Or, simply strike a balance between the two extremes.

Let's look at some examples of character arcs:

- Sarah Connor (*Terminator, 1984 and Terminator 2, 1991*): Sarah starts as a naive waitress at a diner and ends up as a badass soldier who gives birth to the only hope for humankind.

- Shrek (*Shrek, 2001*): At the start of the film, this ogre is tired of people and society rejecting him. He wants nothing more than to be alone in his swamp. By the end of the film, he's a classic hero who has saved the kingdom, found friends, love, and is celebrated by the community that once shunned him.

- Michael Corleone (*The Godfather, 1972*): At the beginning of the film, Michael is fresh out of the military. He wants nothing to do with his family's crime business. He also has the love of a good woman, Kay. By the end of the film, he has committed murders, taken over as head of the crime family, and has alienated Kay.

It is important to note that your hero doesn't have to have an arc. Again, this is a more difficult route to take but is equally satisfying to accomplish. The trick with a "no-arc hero" is that you must have the surroundings change drastically around the character. Instead of the character reacting to their journey, the journey reacts to them. Essentially, their personality is what is sustained while their circumstances change throughout the story.

Let's look at some examples of characters with no arc:

- Jeff "The Dude" Lebowski (*The Big Lebowski, 1998*): The Dude starts as a laid back stoner who likes to go bowling. Nothing bothers him too much. He takes everything in stride or "The Dude abides" as he likes to say. He gets caught up in a roller coaster mistaken identity mystery. But in the end, he hasn't changed (quite literally, goes bowling in the beginning and is bowling at the end).

- Forrest (*Forrest Gump, 1994*): At the start of the film, Forrest is a simple, but sweet-natured man. He lives an extraordinary life but doesn't see himself as extraordinary. This is unique in that there is no real villain in the film. It's Forrest's spirit and good nature that drives the narrative. Times change all around him and he experiences a great deal, but Forrest stays himself despite it all.

- Mark Zuckerberg (*The Social Network, 2010*): At the start of the film, Mark Zuckerberg is a computer genius that can't connect with anyone around him. In starting and running his company, Facebook, he further estranges those closest to him to the point where they sue him. In a way, he becomes the villain of the movie (almost an anti-Forrest Gump). At the end of the film, he is still alone, longing for a connection that he can't achieve.

I'll say it again, your characters are the most important part of your screenplay. From the smallest independent films to the biggest blockbusters, they all have characters you care about. Story and plot mean nothing if the audience doesn't care what happens to the characters within that story and plot. Use the character history sheet I've provided in Appendix A. Dive deep into the characters in your story. Know them. Feel for them. Care about them. The first person who has to relate to your characters is you. You are the first audience. If you don't connect with your characters, no one else will either. It is the screenwriter's job to convince the audience that these people are worth knowing, worth caring about, worth relating to, and worth going on the journey of a film with. If you put in the effort to truly know your characters inside and out, it will also make your writing process infinitely easier. You won't spend time stuck on what a character would do or say in a situation or scene. You'll know because you know them. In a sense, they will cease to be characters in a script for you. They will be real people in a real story. Now all you have to do is write down the story you want them to live.

Chapter 9

DIALOGUE

ere we go! It's the big one! The thing every writer freaks out about! Is it a huge creature attacking the city? No! Is it a nuclear disaster? No! Is it an intergalactic alien invasion? No! It's much worse than all of those things! It's…it's…DIALOGUE! You have a great set of characters with relatable flaws, devastating losses, and satisfying victories. You have an amazing plot with incredible drama, surprising twists, and a mind-boggling ending. Everything is perfect except…what will your characters SAY?! Well, let's all take a deep breath and calm down. I'm here to tell you that dialogue is not as daunting and scary as everyone makes it out to be.

If you've done your character work then you're already halfway done with their dialogue. How? Knowing a character means knowing what they would say at any given moment. You know who they are as people, so all you have to do is ask yourself how that person would react or speak. Let's say your character is a hardened war journalist. You've done the character history for her and you know her as well as any real person. You know she's been all over the world covering war-torn countries. You know she has an ex-husband that has custody of their child. You know she has flecks of gray hair that she's insecure about. You know she's pragmatic and a good problem solver. You know everything there is to know about this person. Now, let's put her in a scene.

She's in a bombed out building. She, along with six refugees, must run across a field to safety. The enemy is dropping bombs on the field every five minutes. So, what does she say? You know she's a problem solver, right? So, she would probably start by taking control of the situation. That means she could say something like, "Everyone, find a partner. Hold hands and don't let go. When the shelling stops, that's when we run. If it starts again, get low and find a place to hide. Does everyone understand? Good. Let's go!" We know that's how she talks because we know her personality. We know her speech patterns. We know she doesn't give up and we know she's got a child to get back to that is likely motivating her actions. See the connection? If you know your characters, you'll instinctively know what they would say and do. Just drop them into the scenes in your plot and let their personality come out in what they say.

Dialogue can also come from real life. Ever overhear something clever in a public place? Write it down. I have pages upon pages of interesting lines I've either overheard or had said to me. Have a clever friend? Listen to what they say and how they say it. Write down any pertinent bits. Pay attention to how people talk. The rhythms of conversations can help you when you write. Eavesdrop. Write everything down. Then, when coming up with characters, you can base the way they talk on a real person. If the real things people say don't fit your scenes, simply make them fit. Change up a funny phrase your dad uses all the time. Add a quirk to the way your neighbor speaks. Real life can be a fertile ground that you can build on.

Speaking of real life, let's talk about conversations. Dependent on culture, conversational rhythms can be very different. For your first script, stick to the type of conversation you are comfortable with. You are used to having conversations within your day-to-day life, so you already have that handled. This is also something that can help when writing dialogue. Unless you live under a rock, you've had plenty of conversations in your life. You already know how people talk. Now you just have to translate that into your writing. When two people are talking, responding to each other is an easy enough way to write. But, that's not always how real conversations are. Sometimes one person is overbearing. Maybe another is afraid to say what they mean. Think about your characters' personality when writing how they speak. Are they a shy person who never speaks up? Or, are they a loudmouth who talks over everyone and expects others to listen. They could be somewhere in between. This is yet another instance of how your characters can inform your dialogue.

If multiple people are speaking at once, it can get harder, but the same rules apply. Is one character sick and tired of never being heard? Then maybe they loudly interject in the middle of a conversation between two others. Perhaps two characters are talking and then one turns their attention to another. Then the others respond to this. This is where rhythm comes into play. When you have conversations, whatever the topic, there is a pace to the conversation. Is your character feeling beaten down at this point in the story? Then perhaps they aren't ready to admit that and they speak slowly and vaguely. Are they angry? Some shouting may be in order. Each of your characters' mental states in the given scene should always be considered when they are speaking. Each character has their own voice. When you have more than two characters in a scene together, consider how each would use, or not use, theirs.

One huge thing to avoid when writing dialogue is characters simply stating how they feel. In real life, no one ever says, "I am feeling regret." If a real person is feeling regret, they may say something like, "I wish I had that day to live over again." Or maybe they are trying to hide their feelings. You've likely encountered an obviously upset person that when asked what's wrong they say, "Nothing." Many times, in real life, the thing people say is actually the opposite of what they really mean or feel. Most people try to avoid embarrassment or shame when they speak. Therefore, most people tailor or change what they say depending on who they are saying it to. Oftentimes, your screenplay will be made better by what is *not said* than what your characters are outwardly expressing. Statements of feeling are unrealistic.

Another mistake that will scream "first time screenwriter" is when every character sounds the same. They all use the same speech patterns and say the same phrases. Avoid this at all costs. Every person speaks differently. Even if they are in the same family or from the same place, they all will have a different way of talking. Be aware of certain phrases or speech patterns that each character uses. All of these should be unique to the character. If you find that multiple characters are using the same words, they need to be changed. Each character has their own personality. With that comes their own unique way of speaking and their own unique vocabulary.

Some screenwriters like to say that they "get the characters talking." This is a good idea. What they mean by this is that they have a general idea of where a scene or conversation is going, but they allow their knowledge of the characters and their individual personalities to lead the dialogue. This is a great way to approach a scene. Often, I have an idea of what the characters want going into a scene but I don't know every word of what they'll say. It may seem a bit odd, but I like to let the character say whatever they want in the moment. In a sense, I let the characters "take over" while I'm writing. If you know your characters enough, you will be able to get out of the way and let them just talk to each other. That is when you come up with the best dialogue. It's when the characters are saying it that it ceases to feel like writing and begins to sound like real speech. This may sound strange, but if you let your characters talk, you will write lines of dialogue that you don't even feel like you came up with. It will feel like the characters just said them. One common thing about creative people is sometimes they feel as if the work is "coming through" them. This is what they mean. It means getting out of your own way. Before or during your writing session, really try to picture the movie in your mind's eye. If you're lucky, you will feel as if you are simply transcribing the movie you are watching in your head. When it comes to screenplays, knowing your characters allows you to get out of their way and let them speak.

Every screenwriter I know and many screenplay books treat dialogue as some sort of gargantuan horror that is to be feared. I'm here to tell you not to worry too much. If you don't want it to be a problem, simply don't treat it as one. Just let your characters speak for themselves. Doing the work to flesh out your characters will make writing dialogue so much easier. Know your characters, know your dialogue. It's that simple.

Chapter 10

SCENE BREAKDOWN

You've come a long way. Now it's time to take the final step before you write a rough draft of the full screenplay. It is now time to break down each scene of the film. Remember that second notepad, it is time to make use of it. Gather your timeline and your scene cards because you are now going to condense them into this one, final document. The reason you make use of the notepad separately is to essentially filter everything down into one place. After this, you will no longer need your many cards, charts, and pads. You will only need the scene breakdown and whatever you use to write the script with. After this, you will write your first real, full draft of the screenplay.

With the timeline and notecards ready, start at scene one. I like to hand write, so I write in all caps: "SCENE 1" and put a box around it. If you're typing, you'll want to at least bold the typeface. I like to go in chronological order, so as I'm working my way through the scenes, I can keep a throughline in my head. After SCENE 1, I write a short summary of the scene from beginning to end. Now, the trick here is to be as basic as possible. Do not use any adjectives (describing words). Be as basic and mechanical as possible, but be thorough. Simply and plainly state what happens in the scene. Use character names and simple actions to let you know what to describe when writing. For example SCENE 1: "Mary argues with her husband. He gets angry. She packs a bag and leaves." That's all you need. Nothing fancy. Just make it understandable, so you can recall the scene when you read it later. Now you're on to SCENE 2: "Mary drives her car to her sister's house. Sad music on car radio." Notice how you can even omit basic grammar if you need to. This breakdown is almost more like a reminder for yourself of the scenes you are going to write in the next step.

I say to keep it simple for a good reason. You don't want to get too descriptive because you want to save that for the script itself. Don't expend too much creative energy on the breakdown. No one cares if your scene breakdown is beautifully written. This is not a document meant for anyone but you. This is your guide to your scenes. In all my years of writing, not a single person has ever read my scene breakdowns. No one should read any of what you have worked on up until this point. Remember, the finished screenplay is all anyone else needs to see. If you were a chef in a restaurant, you'd only give people a prepared meal. You wouldn't take them into the kitchen and show them each ingredient. The same goes for writers. Your notes are just for you. The script is for others.

NOTE: A "scene" in a screenplay is when the location of the action changes. For example, if two people are speaking in the kitchen of a house, then move to the living room. That would be two scenes. One in the kitchen, one in the living room.

In the short descriptions of the scenes, make sure to include everything you want to put in the scene. Character names, actions, any dialogue ideas, etc. Include anything that you have in your notes that will help you articulate the scene. Once again, you'll want to watch the film in your mind as you are thinking of scenes. Put down anything you will need to remember later. One of the main reasons for writing out your scenes in this way is so you can quickly recall the main points of the scenes when you sit down to write a draft of the script. Otherwise, you can waste time trying to remember how a scene was supposed to play out when you thought of it or wrote a scene card weeks ago. The scene breakdown will jog your memory so you can quickly get the scene into the rough draft without leaving any crucial information out.

Another reason for this breakdown is that it forces you to think through the entire script scene by scene. The timeline helps with larger chunks of action. The scene cards help with getting smaller ideas out quickly. The breakdown is where those two components combine. This is when the movie fully comes together in your mind before getting it down on paper. When breaking down scene by scene, pay close attention to how one scene connects to another. This is a crucial part of the breakdown. Perhaps Scene 32 shows your protagonist getting hurt badly and Scene 33 has them with bandages on their face. But, do you need to show them going to the hospital? If so, you can add in a small scene as Scene 33 and re-label the next scene as Scene 34.

Even if you feel like your scene cards and timeline have you covered, thinking through scene by scene can force you to patch holes in your narrative that you may not have realized. The breakdown allows you to consider these decisions before they end up in your screenplay.

Other times, you may want to add or subtract scenes to make the story flow better. For example, maybe you had a sunset scene on a card or in the timeline. But when writing the breakdown you realize that the only reason it was there was to show the passage of time. So now you can cut that scene out and your next scene in the breakdown can take place at night. Additionally, you can also think through the pacing of the scenes once you see them written out back-to-back. Remember reversals? When writing your scene breakdown, you can clearly see if you have too many slow paced scenes in a row or too many fast paced ones. This way, you can switch up the scenes on the fly before they end up in a draft of the script. Trust me, reshuffling your scenes in a breakdown is a great deal easier than rewriting them once they are in the script itself.

A typical scene breakdown for me is between 20-30 handwritten pages on a notepad. That's if I start at Scene 1 and move all the way to the end. My scene breakdowns are about 75-100 scenes long. Your breakdown is for your story, so you can make it however long or short you want. The main thing is to make sure you put in all the relevant information for you to write your rough draft. Keep it simple, but not so simple you have to break out your scene cards to remember the details you need. This document will be your guide throughout the writing of your rough draft, so keep it in a safe place or save it in multiple file locations. Once this is done, you are now ready to write out a fully realized version of your screenplay.

Chapter 11

SCREENPLAY PAGE BASICS

t's time. You made it. Now you're ready to write your first full draft of your screenplay. It's going to be a rough draft that will go through many changes, but it is the first time you're going to write your whole movie from beginning to end. To do this, you'll need to know the basic layout of a screenplay. Let's take a look at what concepts and elements make up a page of a professional screenplay.

Basic Elements Of A Screenplay

Screenplays are written in one font and one size only. Those are: Courier & 12 point. That is it. Nothing else…ever. Why? Standardization. Because Courier is the only font where each letter takes up the same amount of space on the page. Therefore, if every script is written in this font, every 100 page script will be the same length and take the same amount of time to read.

- Screenplays are written on standard 8 ½" x 11" paper. No crazy sizes!

- Unlike novels, screenplays are written in the present tense. When you write a screenplay, you are writing things as they happen. In a novel, you are writing an account of events. For example:

Screenplay: She *runs* into the room. Novel: She *ran* into the room.

Screenplay: He *raises* his voice. Novel: He *raised* his voice.

This is a key difference that separates a screenplay from other writing types. At first, it may feel awkward to make this transition (especially if you are used to writing in the past tense). With enough writing practice, you'll get used to it. Soon, you'll grow to love it. A screenplay feels intensely immediate. You aren't reading about something that happened in the past. It's happening *right now* on the page as you read it.

- Generally speaking, one screenplay page is equal to one minute of screen time in the finished film. 100 page script = 1 hour 40 minute long movie. While some would argue this is not strictly the case, it is an agreed upon standard.

- Your target page count is roughly 100. This can vary, but since this is your first script, be sure to keep it in the 95-105 range. Now, I'm sure you're thinking, "I've seen films that are three hours long." Of course, that is true, but I would wager that few or none of those movies were written by first time writers. When you've won a couple of Oscars and you can write any film you want, then make a three hour long epic. For now, keep it short and simple.

- DO NOT INCLUDE ANY CAMERA ANGLES / EDITING DECISIONS / PERFORMANCE NOTES FOR ACTORS. This is a big one. It is widely misconstrued that a screenplay is about how the film will be shot once it is in production. This is incorrect. What most non-writers think is a screenplay is called a Shooting Script. A shooting script is the final version of the screenplay before it is filmed. This is not what you are writing. The screenplay is the story of the film. Nothing more, nothing less. Do not include anything that can be considered the writer trying to "direct" the movie from the page. Camera shots, editing, and acting choices are not for the writer to make. Leave those decisions to directors, actors, and editors. If you include these things, you might as well stamp the title page of your script with, "Amateur! Don't take me seriously!"

- Avoid long monologues. This is not a stage play. You are not Shakespeare. While a monologue is a good way for an actor to show off their abilities, filmmaking is a visual medium. We want to give the audience something to look at. While they may want to watch Denzel Washington or Meryl Streep give a monologue, those actors are unlikely to star in the first film you write. Having a giant chunk of dialogue in the middle of your script just looks like a big red flag. Keep your dialogue short and to the point. Anything longer than half a page, and you'll either want to shorten it or break it up with some visuals or description of action.

- Avoid long stretches of action description. Just like a monologue, you don't want to cram your script with big blocks of descriptions. This is for two main reasons. Number one, if your film gets made, the director and actors will likely decide how to act out the scene anyway. There is no point in describing each bead of sweat coming off your protagonist's brow if, in the end, the director decides the character isn't sweaty at all. You've just wasted your time writing and the reader's time reading it. Reason number two is closely related: it takes up too much time to read. A screenplay is not a novel (as much as some screenwriters wish they were). A quickly paced script is an exciting script. Big blocks of text on each page will slow your script's pace down to a crawl. Sometimes, certain complex things need a little more description and that's fine. Just don't make it a habit and keep it short whenever possible. My personal goal when describing action is to keep it to four sentences. This is not set in stone, but it's a good guideline to keep in mind.

You'll need to know the basics of script format in order to write a draft. Take a look at this example page from one of my scripts. For context, this is a folk tale set in 1909.

I've numbered the most common script elements you'll need to know. If you've read a screenplay before then these elements will look familiar. While this is not a complete list, anything further is so rare that I have never used it or seen it used. Let's break down their definitions, placement, and use cases for each.

15.

EXT. VILLAGE STREETS-DAY **1**

The next day, Marco makes his way passed the fountain in the village square. He's dressed in his best. He carries a single red rose and bag from the bakery. **2**

He's on his way to the general store to see Adelaide.

FADE TO: **3**

INT. GENERAL STORE-DAY

The place is a proper mercantile. Exposed brick, wooden beams, and animal skins are everywhere. The aisles are so packed with goods they are barely wide enough for a person.

They have everything: food, clothing, tools, pocket watches, firearms, shoes, and anything else one could need.

Marco enters and sees the store's owner, VICTOR (52), behind the counter. He's a mountain of a man with a thick, greasy, black moustache. He wears a tattered denim apron that fit well about fifty pounds ago. **4**

                    MARCO **5**
          Hello, sir. Are you the owner?

                    VICTOR
          That's me. Victor.

                    MARCO
          I'm Marco, Armand's apprentice
          baker. **6**

                    VICTOR
          Ah, yes. The new man in town.

                    MARCO
          Still fresh out of the box. It's a
          pleasure to meet you.

They shake. Marco's hand disappears into Victor's huge mitt.

                    VICTOR
                 (looking at rose) **7**
          For me? You shouldn't have.

                    MARCO
          Not this one. But, I did bring some
          chocolate pastries. I little birdie
          told me those are your favorite.

He sets the bag down and retrieves the pastries.

71

NOTE: On your first page, the words FADE IN in all capitals should be on the first line. Your screenwriting program will likely place it right justified or left justified.

1. Scene Heading aka Slugline: This is how you begin every scene in your script. It consists of three parts: INT or EXT, Location, DAY or NIGHT. INT stands for interior (if your scene takes place indoors). EXT stands for exterior (if your scene takes place outdoors). Then your location, such as Kitchen, Alley, Office, etc. Then DAY or NIGHT to indicate the time of day. I like to capitalize all of my scene headings so they stand out and the scenes are easier to find on the page. Keep these as short as possible. An amateur move is to put too much information in your scene heading. Save extra info for the scene description and only put it in if it's absolutely vital.

Here's an example of what NOT to do when writing your scene headings:

INT. BAR WHERE JOHNNY MET SUZY FOR THE FIRST TIME WHEN THEY WERE IN COLLEGE AND THEY FELL IN LOVE - A QUARTER PAST EIGHT, ABOUT WHEN THE BARTENDERS CHANGE SHIFTS

INT. BAR - NIGHT is how that should read. Then, if you must, put in the other information later in the scene description.

Remember, a new scene (and heading) is needed any time you move to a different location. When picturing it in your mind, imagine a cut in the movie just before every scene heading. This will help you decide if a new scene heading is needed.

Here's a technique I wish I knew a long time ago: When multiple scenes take place indoors, but in multiple rooms of the same space, I use one blanket scene heading at the beginning when the characters arrive at the location. Then I use a capitalized name of the other rooms instead of a scene heading. This is called a Subheader. For example, if I have a character arrive at a house this would be the first scene heading: INT. HOUSE - DAY. Then when the characters move from the living room to the kitchen, instead of writing a whole new scene heading for the kitchen, I would simply write KITCHEN where a new scene heading would normally be. By doing this, you avoid having to clutter up your script with scene headings when your characters are simply moving around an enclosed space. I would not use this technique if they move outside, the scene heading would have to change to EXT. I also wouldn't use it if they are in a large building moving from floor to floor. For that, I would write a new heading for each floor to avoid confusing the reader.

NOTE: There are two special cases where the scene heading may look a bit different. One, if your scene takes place in a car, you need to indicate whether or not the car is in motion. An example of a car scene heading would be INT. TED'S CAR (STOPPED) - NIGHT. If the car is moving, simply put MOVING in the parenthesis. Two, if your action takes place over multiple locations. In this case, use CONTINUOUS in your heading. Meaning the scene is one continuous action. Say you have a character who is walking through a parking garage into a mall, the scene heading could look like this: EXT. MALL PARKING GARAGE - CONTINUOUS. Then you could describe the character's path in the scene description. For your first script, I would avoid using this if possible. It is often misused and can be construed by the reader as the writer directing from the page.

2. Description of action aka Stage Direction: Put simply, this is where you describe what is physically happening in the scene. Be sure to note when characters move through the space, pick up things, make important gestures, etc. The main thing here is to describe things that need to be seen by the audience. What you want to avoid are things the audience *can't* see such as interior feelings and thoughts. Think visually. For example, if your character is getting angry, don't write, "She feels angry inside." But, if you think visually, maybe you could write, "She scowls." See the difference? One the audience can't see, the other they can see. Keep this as simple as possible. You don't want to get too detailed with the writing. Describing words are fine, such as "sprint" instead of "run," just don't describe every step as it hits the ground. Remember a simple directive: IF YOU CAN'T SEE IT ON SCREEN, DON'T WRITE IT.

As mentioned, avoid big blocks of action. If you have a long scene with no dialogue, cut the description down to the absolute bare minimum. If it still feels like too much, group the actions into four sentence pieces. Then separate those pieces with a blank line on the script page between them. After that, if it still feels too long, consider intercutting (cutting back and forth) a dialogue scene with the action. Sometimes, this can improve both scenes.

3. Transitions: This is a cut from one scene to another that is more elaborate than just a simple "cut" in the editing. They are written in ALL CAPS. Depending on your writing software, they will either be on the far left or far right of the page. Let's take a look at the different varieties and their uses:

-FADE IN: Used on the first page of the screenplay to indicate the start of the film.

I use this one on all of my screenplays, but it only goes on the first page. It's an industry standard opening line.

-FADE OUT / FADE TO BLACK: Used on the final page of the script to indicate the film's end.

I also use this one on every script, only on the last page. These first two are the only transitions that appear in every screenplay.

-CUT TO: Meant to be a quick, jarring cut from one scene to another. Often to a new location.

I've never used this one. Avoid.

-BACK TO: Used when cutting back and forth from one location to another.

I use this one exclusively when writing a scene with two people talking on the phone. I use scene headings to establish each location, then use this instead of having to write a new scene heading when each person is speaking.

-JUMP CUT TO: A cut to another space of time (usually forward).

I use this very rarely. It can help when you need to jump forward in time. I've used it when a character is driving to a location we've seen them at before. That way I don't have to bore the audience by showing the character driving.

-DISSOLVE TO: A fade from one scene to another. Used to indicate the passage of time.

I use this one very rarely also. Only when I want to show a significant amount of time has passed, such as a full day or more.

-MATCH CUT / MATCH FADE: When one scene cuts or fades from one image to another that is visually similar or in a similar position. I never use this one. Avoid.

Transitions are yet another facet of screenplays that is debated among screenwriters. Some feel it is "directing from the page" (again). Others feel they are necessary to convey a "cinematic" style (we'll talk about that later). My best advice about the use of transitions is, generally speaking, to avoid them. Most scripts will read just fine without them. If you must use them, do so sparingly. Remember, if you're not sure whether or not a particular change in scenes needs a transition, it's always best to leave it out. An unnecessary or incorrect transition is much worse than one that is simply not there.

4. Character Introduction: Notice that the character of Victor's name is in all caps the first time I introduce him. This is standard and must be done. You only have to capitalize a character's name the first time they appear in the screenplay. I like to include the character's age in parentheses, but this is not strictly necessary.

NOTE: Sometimes in screenplays, you'll see other things capitalized. They include sounds, special effects, visual effects, and props. This is something that appears in a shooting script (again, not what you are writing right now). They are used to denote to the different departments in a film's production what they will be tasked with creating. Some writers will tell you that you must capitalize these things. Others will tell you not to. Personally, when I write a script, I leave them un-capitalized. With the subject so in dispute, I opt to avoid it. Plus, it can become confusing when writing what to capitalize and what not to. My personal feeling is that I'm the writer of the movie, if and when it gets into production, they can figure out what is and isn't important. Directing from the page' should go both ways. If they don't want me to do it, I won't. They shouldn't get to pick and choose when.

5. Character's name above dialogue: This one is simple. It's the name of the character who is speaking. It's always in ALL CAPS and always in the middle of the page.

In some screenplays, there are examples of what's called "parallel dialogue" or "split dialogue." This is when two characters are speaking at the same time. There is usually an option for this buried somewhere in every screenwriting software. Avoid this for your first script. It's a specialized option and you don't need it. Honestly, it's exceedingly rare. I've never used it and have only seen it a few times. If you absolutely must have two characters speak at the exact same time, they should say the same line, like two people yelling "NO!" in a comedy. In this rare case, simply put both of their names over the line of dialogue.

NOTE: Occasionally, to the right of a character's name will be marked with a notation sometimes called an extension in parentheses. These are not to be confused with a parenthetical, which we'll discuss in a bit. These include:

-(O.S.) OFF SCREEN: The character is physically there in the scene, but is delivering lines when the audience can't see them. Example: A visible character says, "Honey, I'm home!" and their unseen spouse replies, "I'm in the garage!" The character in the garage would have (O.S.) next to their name.

-(O.C.) OFF CAMERA: This is an outdated term that means the same as (O.S.) Do not use it.

-(V.O.) VOICE OVER: The character's voice is coming from somewhere outside the scene. Example: A character is telling the story from a point in the future, such as in a detective film. "I had never seen him before, and I could tell I never wanted to again." That character's name would be marked with (V.O.) Another example: If someone is reading a letter and hearing the writer's voice in their head as they read, "Dear Martin, I'm leaving you and taking our pet koala with me." That character would be noted with (V.O.) next to their name.

-(SUBTITLE): This one is self-explanatory. The dialogue is spoken in a foreign language and printed in a subtitle at the bottom of the screen. Personally, when I have used this notation, I like to state what language is being used beforehand in the scene description. Example: Scene description: The man only spoke Korean. CHARACTER NAME (SUBTITLE) "I have to leave!" This way, the reader knows that, on screen, the line will be delivered in a foreign language.

Avoid using these notations if at all possible. Many times, they are not necessary, and will simply clutter your pages. The only one I have ever personally used is (O.S.).

6. Dialogue: The lines of speech that the character is saying. The lines appear under the character's name in the center of the page. Be aware: because it is stacked in the middle of the page, it can fill up pages fast (another reason to avoid monologues). Keep it short when possible, but not at the cost of realism. Underwritten dialogue sounds robotic. Overwritten dialogue sounds like someone sat down and wrote it, not like a real person speaking.

7. Parenthetical: An action or emotional directive for the character. This appears in a small caption in parenthesis below the character name. All of the words are lowercase. They should not exceed four or five words. I recommend avoiding these if you can. They are often perceived as that old pesky nugget "the writer directing from the page." Most every actor and director I know simply disregard them. That being said, there are two very specific situations I use them in. Number one: if I need to get across an action which is so small that it doesn't warrant an entirely separate line of action in the script. Number two: during a rewrite, if I am desperate to cut down the script and I must save some space on the page. A parenthetical takes up less space on the page than a separate line of action. Notice how I didn't mention emotion or acting. Sometimes parentheticals will contain *how* the line should be said. I avoid these altogether. I only use them for action.

If all of these parts feel like a lot to learn, there is no need to worry. Most of it is specialized and only used for specific purposes. All you need to know are the seven main parts I've shown above. Also, if you are handwriting your rough draft, strict formatting isn't necessary. You only need to be able to read it yourself. Once you get to typing up your first draft, your screenwriting program will take the guesswork out with prompts and options that are fairly easy to follow. For example, in Final Draft, after you type a character's name, it will automatically drop the cursor in place to type dialogue. If you're still concerned, here's a quick diagram of the basics:

```
FADE IN (goes here only on the first page)
SCENE HEADINGS GO HERE
DESCRIPTION OF ACTION GOES HERE
      NAME OF SPEAKING CHARACTER GOES HERE
            DIALOGUE GOES HERE
                        TRANSITIONS GO HERE
FADE OUT or FADE TO BLACK(goes here on the
                              last page)
```

That's it. That is basically all you need to know when writing your rough draft. This is the most I've ever needed to learn. Let the screenwriting program take care of the formatting for you once you start typing up a draft.

Chapter 12

ROUGH DRAFT

Time for the fun part: your rough draft! You made it. You're ready. I like to call mine a rough draft because I hand write it. If you type up your rough draft, you can call it a first draft. It's up to you. One of the many great things about writing your rough draft is you don't have to hold back. Let your imagination run wild. Put in every idea you've got. This is the time to get it all out of your system. Every draft after this will be about refining the script. But the first draft is about ideas. Throw everything at the wall. Don't worry about if it's bad or good right now. This brings me to a massively important point. It is one of the most important concepts in this entire book, so I'm going to say it loud:

DO NOT EDIT YOUR ROUGH DRAFT UNTIL IT IS DONE!

There is no greater deterrent to being a writer than second guessing what you are writing as you write it. You can edit it later. You *must* finish it. From beginning to end without *any* editing. Even if you hate every single syllable, you have to keep going until you're done. If you think it's hot garbage, that doesn't matter right now. A garbage script that is written can be fixed. An unfinished script is nothing. I'll let you in on another secret: nobody likes their rough draft. It's a whole lot of fun to write, but it's not anything close to good. No writer worth their salt lets a single other person read their rough draft. The difference between a writer and a wannabe writer is a real writer finishes. Period. They say life is about the journey, not the destination. Well, not in screenwriting. Having a finished script that you can fix later is infinitely more valuable than a stack of 45 pages that are stuck in the second act and will never get done. Even a bad script is a commodity for a writer. It's a thing. It exists. It may be tough to get there, but you must get there.

To get there, you will need that bit of equipment listed way back in Chapter 2: a large, 200 page spiral-bound notebook. Grab that and your notepad with your scene breakdown on it. These are the two items that will carry you to the end of your rough draft. When I write, I simply have these two items and a few pens. Keep your scene breakdown next to you and read each scene's summary before you write it out in full in the notebook.

I like to start at Scene 1 and work my way through chronologically. I begin at the beginning and end at the end. That's just how my brain works. And, for your first script, it can help to give the story a through-line in your mind as you write. I once heard that you should think of your scenes as pieces of metal and your ending as a magnet. I think about that a lot when writing.

That said, the actual process of writing is as individual as the writer. So, if you prefer, write whatever scenes you like in what order you like. If you've got an absolutely crystal clear version of the ending scene in your head and you just have to get it out first, go for it. I'm not going to stop you. I don't do this because sometimes I find that the scenes don't fit together so well if I write them out of order. It can cause a scattered effect that I find confusing. To each their own.

NOTE: Page numbers mentioned for your rough draft are noted for a handwritten draft. If you choose to type your rough draft, decrease the page numbers by half.

Opening Scene

Let's talk briefly about opening scenes, or "hook" scenes. Some films start with a scene that grabs the audience's attention right away, or "hooks them in" (hence the name). These scenes are often used to start the movie off with some excitement. That is why they are most common in action films. An opening scene full of stunts, gunfire, and explosions can get the audience's attention quickly. But, a good opening hook scene can do more than simply provide some cheap thrills before diving into the story. A good opening scene can serve many purposes such as introducing the hero, the villain, character relationships, or the world your screenplay takes place in. I like to establish the world and setting and introduce my main character in the first scene. That tells the audience quickly "here's who you should pay attention to and here's the world they live in." If I can throw in some excitement or action, that is icing on the cake.

Examples of films with great opening scenes:

- *Children of Men (2012)*: Establishes the main character and a chaotic, futuristic world (all in one shot, no less).

- *The Lion King (1993)*: Introduces us to the characters and the relationships that will affect the rest of the story. Also hits us with the beauty of the setting and music.

- *No Country for Old Men (2007)*: Introduces the protagonist in voiceover. Shows the villain, what he's capable of, and the violent world the characters inhabit.

Act 1

You've written FADE IN on your first page. Now what? In the first 20 pages or so, I like to set up my world and characters. The first scenes should be mostly about settings and people. Think about the kind of environment your film will take place in. Picture it in your mind as you write. Is your world dangerous? Silly? Oppressive? Use your first scenes to establish this. If at all possible, do so visually rather than with unnatural sounding dialogue. For example, if cold weather is going to be a part of your world, don't have a character simply say, "It's cold." Instead, describe a frost on the windows that is there eight months out of the year. This way, you can evoke a picture in the reader's head that allows them to get a feel of your world. If you simply state things, it doesn't allow room for the reader to picture it.

When you're introducing characters, there are many ways to describe them so that you capture their essence or spirit for the reader. Be sure to describe them with more than just what they are wearing. Just as in real life, a person's character is more than just how they look. You can get into their personality a bit, where they work as it applies to the story, their demeanor, etc. Are they bright and approachable, or not to be messed with? Perhaps they look scary, but they're actually friendly and this can come into play later in the plot. The only time I get into what the person is wearing is when it applies to the story or reveals something about the person. In the example page, I introduce the character Victor by describing his apron. But, I don't just say, "He's wearing an apron." That wouldn't tell us much about him. I say the apron "fit well fifty pounds ago." That is something he's wearing, but the description reveals aspects of his character: he's worked at the job a long time (since he was a thin man) and he doesn't care much about his looks. You want to avoid descriptions that don't reveal anything.

Introducing the characters and the world should take up the first 10-15 pages. If you can do it in fewer, go for it. Now is the time that something needs to happen to change the character's trajectory in the story. This is often called "the inciting incident." I don't love this term, because it implies there needs to be some kind of big "event" to cause a character to take action. This isn't always the case. It can be something big or small. From a life changing car crash to picking a flower in a garden, almost anything can be an inciting incident. I prefer the term "story catalyst." It just needs to mean something to the character and make them examine and change where they are going. It needs to push them into the story.

You've got your main characters set up. The world and settings are feeling good. An event shifted the character's path. Now, with your next 20 or so pages, you want to set up the main conflict of the movie. You don't have to dive deep into it yet, but you want to establish what it is and what the stakes are. Is your main character thinking about robbing a bank? Getting divorced? Flying off into space? This is the time when they need to start weighing the decision within themselves and with others. This also allows the reader and audience to start thinking about the pros and cons of the character's decisions. Remember, your main character is your audience's guide through the story. When they feel something, the audience needs to feel it as well. In these pages, there needs to be something coming. An obstacle. What do they want? What is stopping them from getting it? These things need to materialize on the page at this point. Often, the villain is the one supplying the obstacles. So, now is the time for them to put their evil plan into motion. In terms of act structure, these pages constitute the end of Act 1. This is the time to set up the conflict and obstacles that will make up the majority of Act 2.

Act 2

This one can be a pain. Often, it can be easy to know how to start a story and how to end one, but what happens in between? How do you connect them? The way I like to think about it is Act 2 is the action of the story. This act should build on everything that came before it. At the beginning of Act 2 is when your character or characters needs to commit to whatever the main events of the story are. Is your main character driving across the country to meet the parent they never knew? Now is the time when they start driving. Opening a restaurant? Now is when they start buying kitchen equipment and cleaning up the place. Tracking down an escaped killer? This is when the cop finds a major clue. You get the picture. The start of Act 2 is when the main plot point takes effect. Shortly after this is when the character runs into their first major obstacle. The car won't start for the road trip, the restaurant has rats, and the cop just got saddled with a rookie partner. Additionally, the villain should be taking their plans up a notch right about now. Act 2 is about action.

Act 3

This is the climax of everything. This is when the story resolves itself. The beginning of this act is when the hero should suffer the most. Your characters need to be at their lowest point to make their redemption at the end the most impactful it can be. Let's stick with our examples. On the road trip, the car engine explodes and the hero has no money to fix it. Opening night of the restaurant went horribly, they got a bad review from a prominent food critic, and no more customers are coming in. The cop confronted the killer but they killed the rookie partner and disappeared. Remember, the more your character suffers, be it emotionally or physically, the better it will feel for the character and audience when the suffering ends.

After the character has hit bottom, you have to bring them back up (or at least affect some sort of catharsis). This is the point where everything comes to a head. The stakes are the highest they've ever been or will be. This is the height of the trajectory of the story. Everything has come to this. Let's look at our examples once more. The hero hitched a ride and has made it to their long lost parent's home. Now it's time to have the big cathartic discussion or argument. The restaurant? Our hero traveled the world and learned to cook a whole new menu. Now, it's the grand re-opening, and the critic is eating the new menu. Our cop? They've tracked the killer to their lair. But, it's dark and confusing. The killer has the upper hand in their final showdown. It's time to roll out any great ideas you have for the finale. Don't hold back, use your best ideas now. Throw everything at the wall. It's the climax of your story! Make it as creative as you possibly can! The truth of the matter is the thing people remember most about a movie is the ending. Put in the most effort you can here and make sure your climax is a memorable one.

You're almost done with Act 3. But now you have to give the audience a little breather. They need a little time to process and wrap up what they've just watched. At this point, the excitement has died down. The hero has made their journey. It's time to leave the audience with a parting note. What was the aftermath of the finale? Let's take one final look at our examples for some ideas. The hero has confronted their long lost parent and they made peace (or not) and now they have to head back home and resume their normal life. Do they keep in touch? It depends on if you want a happy ending or not (contrary to popular belief, you don't have to have a happy ending). The restaurant got a good review and customers are coming back. Will they open a second location? Up to you (and the characters). The cop? He put the notorious killer behind bars and made peace with the rookie's widow. Is it time to retire, or take on another case? Let the cop decide. How you wrap up your story is completely up to you. Don't let anyone, including me, tell you that you have to put a nice bow on everything. You're allowed to leave things ambiguous, or even messy, as long as it makes sense for the story you're telling.

There is one more option for the end of Act 3. It's what I like to call the "non-wrap" ending. After the climax, the film can just end. Roll credits. You don't *have* to wrap it all up and give the audience a breather if you don't want to. Sometimes, when the road trip has been made, the restaurant is re-open, or the killer is dead, there's no more story to tell. It is all dependent on the emotional rhythm and weight of the story. You have to be the judge of that. Now, don't do the non-wrap ending out of laziness. It can be easy to think your script is done when the finale is over. But, you have to be honest with yourself. Is there more story to tell or not? Does the story feel complete? If so, great. You're all done. If not, you've got a bit more work to do. This is why the non-wrap ending can be more difficult to pull off. You have to make the call. Do what feels right on this rough draft. You can change it in another draft if need be (we'll get to that in a bit).

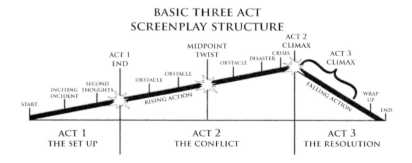

BASIC THREE ACT
SCREENPLAY STRUCTURE

This is a graph of what a traditional screenplay structure looks like. You'll find it in every screenwriting book (and now it's in this one, too). Notice that it looks slightly different from what I've been describing.

I am including it as a mere guideline. I would actually recommend that you deviate from this whenever you feel like it. The problem with most of these formulas (and there are tons of them) is that they make everyone write the same screenplay over and over again. Have you ever seen a movie that was just like another you saw a week ago? Chances are the writers of those films read all the same screenwriting books and looked at too many graphs like the one above. There are some basics to abide by (format, page counts, font size, etc.). The difference is those things are not creative decisions about your story. They are just technical requirements for any screenwriter. Be wary of any formula or secret that tries to dictate your creative decisions. That's when you run into a lack of individual creativity. So, when it comes to structuring your screenplay, the graph above is only to help you visualize the general trajectory of your story. You don't have to follow it to the letter. In fact, please don't.

Here are some final thoughts to keep in mind when writing your rough draft:

1. **Finish!** You have to push through to the end. Don't stop. Even if you know you can do better. You can do better on your next draft. Finish. It's the most important thing about writing, bar none.

2. **Do not edit while writing!** If you start editing before you're done, you'll never finish. Make changes later. A sentiment I once heard was: "During your first draft, you are simply throwing sand into the sandbox. You make the sandcastles later." This is true.

3. **Know your characters, know your dialogue.** Get out of the way of your characters and let them talk. Soon, you'll just be writing down what they say, not straining to come up with something. Let them react to the situations you put them in. Let them live and breathe.

4. **Get it all out of your system.** Put in every idea, character, subplot, etc. you have into this draft. It's the only time when you don't want to be compact and concise. Don't go overboard, but wring

out your scene breakdown and notes. Remember: it's always easier to trim down a long screenplay than it is to add to one that is too short.

5. **Forget about perfection.** The script you have in your head and the script you write will never be a perfect match. That's okay. Many first time writers put too much pressure on themselves in this regard. Every writer has this issue. Even Academy Award Winning screenwriters (whose movies are already filmed and released) wish they could go back and change the script. When you're a writer, you will never get it exactly right, especially not the first time. Accept this fact and move on. Move ahead. Write more.

6. **Pacing.** Keep the energy of your script moving. Switch up your pacing often (every 10 to 15 pages). They should build on each other but a scene or small grouping of scenes should change the pace of the script regularly. Accordingly, each act will have a slightly different pace as well. Remember reversals? Use them and use them well.

At first, your rough draft can seem intimidating. Trust me, I get it. There's no need to feel pressure about it. The beauty of this process, and why you do so much prep work, is to let the process get out of the way and let your creativity loose once it's time to actually write the script. If you do your prep work, you don't have to struggle through a rough draft where you can't think of what to write. You've got your story, you've got your characters. They are there in your mind. They are there in your notes. They are part of you now. There's no need to stress while writing. Use your scene breakdown as your guide and you'll be just fine.

The rough draft is my favorite part of the whole process. It's where you can have fun and put in every idea you have. There is nothing better than sitting down with pen and paper (or computer) and letting your creativity loose like a pent up wild animal. You can put every scene, line of dialogue, and character you've had during this process into this draft. Got a scene you think might be too crazy? Throw it in!

Got a side character you love but aren't sure audiences will connect with? Go for it! This is the draft no one will read but you. You have no critics right now. Right now, it's only you and your creativity. This draft is about getting your thoughts out, not perfecting them. Wring out every one you've got. There are no limits here.

An important thing to note is that you don't have to treat your scene breakdown like it's written in stone. If, during a writing session, you come up with a new scene, a new character, or a new plotline, absolutely put it in. Never think that because it isn't in your notes that you should avoid it.

Always let the story and characters guide you. Remember what I said about dialogue? It is best when you feel like you're getting out of the way of the characters and transcribing what they are saying. The same goes for the story when writing your rough draft. If the story feels like it wants to go in a certain direction, follow it. If characters say things you weren't expecting, let them speak. Never turn yourself off to ideas when writing, even if the ideas that come to you aren't anywhere in your notes. When you let the story and characters guide your writing, odds are what you put on the page will be good. Some of the best writing I've ever done deviated from what I had planned. It can be surprising, even frightening. But it's also exciting. And if it excites you as the writer, there's a good chance it will excite readers and audiences as well.

Chapter 13

FIRST DRAFT: TYPE IT UP, CUT IT DOWN

Congratulations! You did it! You have a draft. You've accomplished more than most people who claim to be writing a screenplay. You finished it. You *have* written a screenplay (even if it's still in its rudimentary form). What now? Move on to the next draft, right? Not so fast. There are three things you should do before you get on with your next draft. First, you should celebrate. Get yourself a little something. Have a tiny party. For me, I like to either get myself a nice meal, a fancy coffee drink or have a celebratory drink with those closest to me. Your rough draft is an accomplishment that should be commemorated. You've earned it. The second thing you should do is take a bit of time off from the script. This allows you to get some semblance of objectivity when you return to it to make changes. If you just plow ahead with your next draft right away, you won't be able to pinpoint what you want to change. It becomes easier to fix up your script once you've had some time away from it. You'll be less precious about things and be more honest with yourself about what needs improvement. I like to take a week to 10 days off from a script once I have a rough draft. This doesn't mean you can't write during this time. If you so choose, work on some other projects in the meantime. The amount of time is up to you. The main thing is to notice when you are no longer thinking about the script on a daily basis. The day I don't think once about my rough draft is the day I know it's time to get back to it.

What about the third thing? Once you've taken some time off for objectivity, you have to read through your rough draft. I read through mine twice. After that, you should make some notes. Personally, because I hand write in a notebook, I like to make my notes in the page margins. I grab a red pen and make notes like an English teacher. These notes don't have to be too in depth for now. A lot of the times, I am merely noting *what* I think needs to be changed or improved. Not *how* I plan on changing or improving. Almost always with these notes, I don't yet have an idea what I'm going to change things to, I just know they need to be changed. More often, the notes will simply be a red circle around something with the words "change" or "improve." If I do have the good fortune of coming up with something on the spot while making notes, I'll write that instead.

There have been times when I was in a hurry to finish and I simply didn't have the time to make notes in the margins of my rough draft. So, when typing up the script for my first draft, I made the notes on the fly. Now, this is not my preferred way to do it, but if you're pressed for time (or simply prefer this method) feel free to use this technique. Be aware, though, that it may not be as thorough as putting your notes in the margins. Another method is something in between: use another notepad to quickly jot down your thoughts when reading through your rough draft.

Alright, you've read through your script a couple of times (or more), you've made some notes, and you have a general idea of where you want to make some changes. Good work! It's now time to type it up. Fire up your computer and open up the screenwriting software of your choice. Keep your notated rough draft next to you and start on page one. What I like to do is simply type up everything I've written and incorporate my notes as I'm typing. If an idea strikes while you're typing that you don't have in your notes, again, this is fine. Put it in. Later on, we'll look at specific aspects each individual draft will focus on. For now, just change anything you want, as long as it is an improvement.

The main goal of typing up the script like this is to simply have a professional version of it. A real First Draft. The handwritten version is just for your personal use. You won't need it once you have a typed version. It has served its purpose. Think of it as a chrysalis that your butterfly of a screenplay used to live in.

This is sort of an evolved version of your rough draft so "improvement" is a broad statement. For me, it's anything that is made clearer. Even better is a change that clarifies something and does so in fewer words. The changes I commonly make while typing the first draft are to simply shorten things as much as I see fit. This means cutting down the description of the action in most scenes. This is a good way to shorten your script quickly. When you read through your rough draft, you'll often find you can describe the same thing in fewer words. With long descriptions for example, my note simply says, "Condense."

Also, if possible, I'll cut down dialogue here and there. One thing to look for specifically is repeated words in dialogue among different characters. What I mean is, often without noticing, you'll have two or more characters speaking similarly. Little phrases at the beginning of lines like, "Oh, well," "I guess," or "Sure, but…" These are common mistakes that can make your characters sound alike (which you don't want). To this day, I catch myself writing the same opening words to some dialogue and have to root it out later. These are the two most common changes I make from the rough draft to the first draft.

What I don't do in this draft is remove any full scenes or characters. At this point, you don't want to make any large, sweeping decisions that can affect the story too much. The reason is that, after this, you will be using this typed version of the script to make changes. If you remove something that you find out later you need, you can save yourself the time of digging out your rough draft and crowbarring those scenes or characters back into the script.

The main takeaway here is that after this draft you will have a typed, professional looking screenplay. Starting at page one and pushing through to the end is more important than notes and improvements at this point. Don't worry about page count and formatting for the time being. It's okay if you have some spelling and grammar errors or your script is 130 pages long (speaking from experience here; my first script was a horrid 148 pages.). These are issues you can fix in the coming drafts. Just get it typed up. Make the changes you want as you go, but don't get too caught up with that yet. You need a workable draft right now, not a perfected draft. There are still plenty of opportunities to make changes.

And that's that. You have a proper, professional draft of your screenplay. If someone asks if you've ever written a screenplay, you can confidently answer, "Yes." If they ask if they can read it, you can insecurely say, "No," and run in the opposite direction. Now you're acting like a real writer! The point is you have…something. You have some castles in the sandbox, the dough to make the bread, bullets in the gun, or whatever other analogy you want to use. Well done! This is itself another big accomplishment. Now, all you have to do is take it from something to something…good. That's what rewrites are for.

Chapter 14

SECOND DRAFT: STRUCTURE

Your first draft of your script looks professional. It's formatted correctly (for the most part). It is in the right font (Courier). Everything is in the right size (12 pt). But, chances are it's a little rough right now. That's perfectly okay. It's still in its early form. No one gets it perfect the first time. It's okay to hate your first draft. So, what can you do? Now is when you need to change your mindset. When crafting the story and writing the rough and first drafts, you need to think in an additive manner. You're creating. You're making. You're adding to the story. You need to start thinking in a subtractive manner. You need to start thinking about what you can remove. You need to start thinking about refining your story. The best place to start is the script's structure. What are the scenes you have and what can you remove without disrupting the story's integrity? In an ideal screenplay, if you take out one scene, the story would make no sense. And if you added a scene, it would stand out as unnecessary. This is why structure is important. This is why it's something you should tackle in this early draft. It is foundational to your screenplay.

Defining Structure

You might be wondering why we're starting with structure instead of dialogue or something else. The main reason is that you don't want to put in work you don't have to. Cutting out scenes helps you get to the core of the story and lets you see where the work needs to be done. Writing a feature screenplay takes long enough, we don't want to spend time rewriting the dialogue in a scene that we end up cutting out later. Working on structure is the quickest way to get your script into a lean and mean shape before putting in the work on what you have left.

When I say "structure," I simply mean the order in which your scenes are placed. This dictates the pace at which you reveal information to the audience. I like to think of my structure like a puzzle that has too many pieces. Think of each scene as a puzzle piece. The trick is to fit all of the pieces together so the picture comes together while getting rid of the pieces that don't fit. The first step during this rewrite is to read through your script and find out which scenes can be cut out. Nearly every first draft has scenes you can lose. I usually cut about 10-20% of my scenes during this draft. The scenes you'll run into most that need to be cut are redundant scenes. These scenes either tell the reader information they already know or summarize information that doesn't need to be repeated. Often, especially with first time writers, they feel the need to rehash or restate the plot because they are worried the audience isn't following it. I am guilty of this myself. There's nothing wrong with overwriting like this during the first draft, but now we need to identify and eliminate these scenes. Read through your script and keep an eye out for repetition of plot information.

Another way to cut down on the sheer number of scenes in your script is to see if you can combine scenes. Often, you can find scenes with complementary information. For example, let's say you're writing a thriller. Your main character buys guns from a dealer at a pier, then three scenes later, gets a contract from his employer at a diner. Why not have the employer also be at the pier? Or at the diner, the gun dealer is in the parking lot and sells the guns there? You'll often find that scenes that felt like they should be separate when you were writing your first draft can be combined quite easily. This is what I mean by thinking in a subtractive way. Combining and compressing scenes like this is how you can cut down your scene and page count fast.

When working on structure, it is also important to look at how each scene connects to the one before it and the one after it. Do they flow together well? If you picture the movie in your mind, do these scenes feel like a logical progression? Do they push the plot forward? Think about your rhythms. Do the scenes all feel like they are paced the same? If so, change it up. Sometimes, you'll find that a scene is simply in the wrong place in the story. Does the suspense packed shootout feel like it happens too late? Try moving it up a scene or two. What if it came later? This is your world, so feel free to mix things up if you feel they aren't working. If I like a certain scene has to happen at a certain time in my script, I move it around and many more puzzle pieces fall into place. Don't allow yourself to become locked into how you previously thought the story had to play out. You have to acknowledge that the story on the page may not match the story in your head. If so, change whatever you want. Nothing is set in stone right now. Think of the big picture you're creating. If one piece doesn't fit in the puzzle in one place, you may find it fits perfectly in another.

Cutting Scenes

What about cutting scenes? What if you can't combine, change, or switch out a scene? How do you know if you should cut the whole thing out? While there may be no one size fits all answer, I'll tell you the closest thing that I have come up with. I call it The Boil Down. This is when you read through a scene a few times and you figure out what is the bare minimum information that this scene must convey to the audience. You "boil it down" to its essence. It might be an action that a character takes. It might be a piece of revealing dialogue. Whatever the case, try to cut through what you've written on the page and see what *must* be written on the page. What is needed for the story to make sense from here? The information conveyed must push the story forward in some way. There should be a sense of momentum in each scene. If you boil down your scene to its bare essential information and it doesn't feel like that information is pushing the narrative forward, that's when you know you should cut the scene. Be honest with yourself. Does the scene advance the story by giving the audience or a character new information, or do you just like the scene because you think it's cool? It's okay to put in a scene that you think is cool when writing your first draft. But this isn't your first draft, is it? It's your second draft. If a scene isn't pulling its narrative weight, get that thing out of there.

Plot Holes

Another issue to look out for during this rewrite is plot holes. Let's take a look at a basic definition:

Plot Hole: In fiction, a plot hole, plothole, or plot error is a gap or inconsistency in a storyline that goes against the flow of logic established by the story's plot. Such inconsistencies may include illogical, unlikely, impossible events and statements or events that contradict earlier events in the storyline.

What does all that mean? Basically, it means you need to keep a logical throughline in your screenplay. Plot hole examples: if the villain in your script has been portrayed as all powerful but is then easily defeated by the hero at the end of the movie. Or if your hero obtains an ancient artifact that is the only way to thwart an apocalypse, then they don't use the artifact when the time comes, yet stop the apocalypse anyway.

The thing about plot holes is they tend to pop up later in the script. Essentially, the rules you set up for your story are established in the early pages of your screenplay. While the resolution to the story is always in the later pages. The problem can arise when resolving the story as you can sometimes contradict your own story without realizing it. Don't beat yourself up about this. Often, you wrote the beginning a long time ago and you may have forgotten a line of dialogue or action from the early part of your script. This is why we re-read the script and do rewrites. The cause for a plot hole rarely rears its ugly head on page 80. It's the plot point you made on page 13 that will come back to bite you in the end. If you run into this situation, you have to make a judgment call. Do you change the later plot point to fit the earlier established rule, or do you change the earlier point to fit the ending? For me, I usually go back to the beginning and make the change. Since scenes should be building on each other, the ending scene will carry more weight, and therefore be more important to the story as a whole. A change at the beginning of the story is usually less harmful than at the end. For example, your characters are in trouble and should have simply called the authorities early on but didn't. Now you have to go back to the start of the script and mention that there are too many corrupt cops in the town to do so. That way, at the end of your script, you can avoid the plot hole of the audience asking, "Why didn't they just call the cops a long time ago?"

Don't be intimidated by structure. Keep your story in mind and re-arrange or cut out any scenes that aren't working. This draft is about trimming away what isn't needed. Keep an eye out for plot holes and inconsistencies. You know your story. Watch it back in your mind as you read your script and remove or change anything you feel the need to. If there is one thing to take away during this or any subsequent draft it's this: when in doubt, cut it out.

Chapter 15

THIRD DRAFT: CHARACTER

Character? We already worked on character, didn't we? Yes. We shaped your characters and worked on their histories. With this draft, we are going to focus solely on character consistency. We need to make sure that our characters don't act out of step with what we have established and what we know about them. One of the worst things a character can do is something wildly out of character in order to make the plot work. I'm sure you've all seen a movie where, right around the start of the third act, a character does something that makes you go, "Huh? Why did they do that?" They do something that goes against everything we know about them leading up to it. The worst offender is the formerly rigid character who comes around to another way of thinking. The alcoholic father who quits drinking to become a family man. The resistant love interest who suddenly falls for the protagonist. The Scrooge who now is filled with the spirit of Christmas. These examples can be done well, but a lot of times the change in character feels unearned, forced, or too quick. The way to do them well is to have a consistent character who goes through a change gradually throughout the film. A series of events that have a cumulative effect on the character. In other words, a character arc. That's what this draft is all about: making sure your characters have consistent arcs, or if they have no arcs, their character traits remain constant.

An exercise I like to do is to pick out a few scenes in the script that are most impactful for a character's arc. These are the scenes where events change the character in some way. There should be at least two scenes where the character is different afterward, either in a major way or something more subtle. It can vary by character. Most likely, your main character will have more. My main characters tend to average about five character arc scenes in the script. Once you have those scenes picked out, write short names down for each along with their page number on index cards or post-it notes. Then you arrange those notes in order as they appear in the script. How does the arc look? Is it a logical progression over the course of the story? Do the events in the scenes feel like they are ramping up in weight and meaning? Is the arc paced well (changes to the character happening too fast or not fast enough)? The answers to these questions should be: good, yes, yes, and yes. If those aren't your answers, you have some rewriting to do. If this is the case, dive back into those scenes during this draft. This is why you note what page they are on. Fix them up by keeping in mind how that scene can better fit into the overall character arc you've established.

Another tip on character arcs: make sure the change in character matches the events in the scenes. For example, let's say your character is a rich man who has decided to cut a certain child out of his will. One of your "arc scenes" is he stubs his toe on a table and then all of a sudden decides to change his mind and include the child in the will. That is not a great match in terms of the weight of the scene's events vs. the weight of the change in the character. The logic doesn't track. Now, if you were rewriting that scene, perhaps he could stub his toe and remember when his son was a toddler and did the same thing. Then the rich man remembers his son cried and he consoled him and they had a beautiful father and son moment. Then the rich man starts to cry just like his toddler did so many years ago. This is the moment when he has a change of heart and decides to reinstate his son into his will. Now that is a scene where the weight of the events in the scene matches the weight of the character change.

One thing I like to do once I reach this stage is to read a character's introduction (on whatever page that occurs) and then read the page with their last appearance in the script. If this is the protagonist, it tends to be on the first and the last pages of the script. Does it seem logical that the earlier character changed into the one at the end? I like to start with the main character and work my way down the list of characters in order of importance to the story. I make a note of any character that needs changing or improvement.

At this point, I then go through the script and make sure that none of the characters' actions feel odd or out of place when compared to who I want the character to be and what I've set them up as. The way to test this is to ask yourself whether an action a character takes or a line of dialogue they say is natural to the character or you are simply forcing them to advance the plot. As an example, let's say your protagonist is a bank robber who must confess to their crimes or their innocent sibling will take the fall. Now, if the character is established throughout the script as a hyper-intelligent criminal mastermind who hates cops, they wouldn't just go to a police station and turn themselves in without a plan. They are too smart to do such a thing. That would be out of character. But, they need to confess to advance the plot while also maintaining consistency of character. Perhaps they could send a confession letter to the sibling's captors just before getting on a plane to a country with no extradition policy. Or, they could confess but then set a trap for the pursuing detectives. These are ways you don't compromise the character while still advancing the plot forward.

You have to come up with creative solutions to hide how you are advancing the plot with your characters' actions and dialogue. Always allow the character's personality to guide the decisions. If you are stuck at how to advance the plot, simply ask how the character you have built would react to the situation. How would they advance the plot if they were in charge of their own story? Where do they want to go from here? When you let character inform your story, advancing the plot becomes easier. Much like dialogue, if you as the writer can get out of the way of what the character wants, you can use how they are as people to advance the story in ways that are unique for the screenplay reader and audience. You can once again just be along for the ride as you let them take over, which always produces the best writing.

On your Character Draft, you'll need to accomplish a few simple goals. First, keep your characters' actions and dialogue in line with the people they are as you've established them. The second goal is to keep their character arc consistent by tracking it throughout the scenes in which the character changes. Lastly, don't merely use your characters as tools for advancing the plot. If you achieve these goals with everyone significant in your script, from your protagonist on down, you'll have characters that feel real and compelling. This holds true for readers and audiences, whether it's your family and friends, a Hollywood executive, or a movie theater full of people.

Chapter 16

FOURTH DRAFT: DIALOGUE

During this draft, you're going to focus solely on the dialogue. Since you've done your work on structure, there shouldn't be any scenes left to cut out of the script. That means it's time to edit what everyone says. The main purpose this time is to once again cut out any lines that don't serve a purpose (push the plot forward and/or reveal character). You'll also want to compress the dialogue and cut out any particularly wordy bits (trust me, they're there). The idea when cutting down dialogue is to get the pieces of dialogue down to their most compact yet impactful form. What you want to do is to strike a balance between compressing the lines while still keeping them sounding real. This is the point of this rewrite: cut out the excess lines, increase the impact of the lines, and make sure they still sound natural.

What should be cut? You can answer this by asking yourself another question: Are the characters speaking to each other or the audience? If it's the audience, cut it out. What I mean is that a lot of times, especially in early drafts, dialogue is simply there to fill in the audience. It is not a natural way of speaking for the character, but they are simply conveying information. The way you can tell this is by what other characters there are in the scene. Do the other characters in the scene already know this information? If the answer is yes, then the character is simply explaining things to the audience. When considering whether to keep or cut dialogue, especially dialogue that clarifies the plot, make sure that it sounds natural and makes sense for the character to say it out loud to others.

Also cut or change dialogue if it is inconsistent with the character. Would the character actually say it and in that way? Is what they are saying true to the character that is in the rest of the script? If the answer is no, cut it out. Again, you have to be honest with yourself. Don't keep a line in because you like it or think it's cool. Every writer is guilty of adding lines simply because they like them. But if the line doesn't fit the character, it ceases to be a good line. Be honest with yourself and true to your story. Don't just cram cool lines into a character's mouth when that isn't the way they would really talk.

The next task of this draft is to cut down any wordy bits of dialogue. What I mean by this is when you made your character say too many words to get the point across. This is problematic for two reasons: 1. It makes your screenplay longer than it needs to be. 2. Your character doesn't sound like a real person if they speak with too many ornamental words. You can correct these problems with two questions: 1. Does this dialogue push the narrative forward and/or reveal character? If the answer is no, cut that mess out of there. 2. Does this dialogue sound like a person talking or do they sound too much like a movie character? The answer here should be "real person." Often, through no fault of your own, you can find yourself writing dialogue that sounds like "movie speak." This is when your character starts saying things that would never, ever happen in the real world. They speak in movie catchphrases and one-liners that are meant to sound cool or clever to an audience but have little relation to how a person speaks in reality. The reason for this is chances are you've seen a lot of movies by the time you decide to write one. So, instinctively and without realizing it, you'll write something that belongs in a movie. This is not what you want (unless maybe you're writing some kind of parody, which we aren't right now). What you want is realism. You need to know how to write realistically because this is the bedrock of writing. Once you can write realism, you are free to go into other forms from there. But you need that baseline knowledge first. To achieve this, use your character work as a sounding board for the dialogue. Be honest with yourself and ask if the character is speaking or if it's you, the writer, trying to sound cool. It's okay to admit this to yourself. You really have to. There have been many times when I had to cut a line of dialogue, sometimes my favorite line in the entire script, because I had to confess to myself that it didn't fit the character. If you love the line and are convinced it belongs in a movie, write it down in your notes. Label that note page "Dialogue Ideas" and add to it whenever you have an idea for an interesting line for a movie. Soon, you'll have a huge collection of pre-written dialogue that may fit a character you write in the future.

Just because a puzzle piece doesn't fit into this puzzle, doesn't mean it won't fit one in the future.

When it comes to cutting dialogue, I like to think of it as pruning branches off of a tree. You're cutting the excess to strengthen what is left over. In the same way, when you cut down dialogue, you can shorten your script and make what dialogue is left in more effective. A theory that illustrates this well is Ernest Hemingway's "Theory of Omission aka The Iceberg Theory." Hemingway states, "If a writer of prose knows enough about what he is writing about he may omit things that he knows and the reader, if the writer is writing truly enough, will have a feeling of those things as strongly as though the writer had stated them. The dignity of movement of an ice-berg is due to only one-eighth of it being above water." Essentially, what he means is that if you write in a simple, effective manner, the reader will be able to picture what the writer is trying to convey in their mind. This is what is meant in screenwriting terms as "writing visually." For an author of books like Hemingway, it simply means that they let the audience fill in the image of what the writer intends. For screenwriters, this means that the writing can allow the reader to picture it but also allows room for a director to interpret the script when creating images for the screen. Remember the pesky thing of "directing from the page?" Writing visually is the acceptable way to do that. If your images are strong enough, the director will create something close to what you intended in the script. When it comes to dialogue, this is often useful when thinking about how real people speak. In real life, people don't break out into extravagant speeches where they confess their innermost thoughts and feelings (that's what stage plays are for, zing!). Most often in real life, what's most revealing about how people speak is what they *don't* say. Use this to your advantage when cutting down your dialogue in this draft. What if your character could say what they're feeling with a look? What if what they are trying to say is boiling inside of them but is too hard to say, so they blurt out something completely ridiculous for the given situation? What if they say they are feeling the opposite of what they are showing in body language? Putting things like that in your script instead of a wordy, unnecessary monologue will greatly improve your dialogue while allowing you to cut down your page count.

When it comes to your dialogue draft, just remember to shorten and strengthen. What you want is for the spoken words to be as few as possible with the most amount of impact. Most of the times, you'll find you can have a character say the same with fewer words. Along with that comes an added weight to each word. If your character's words are compact and lean, chances are they will convey their meaning with more efficacy. Remember: you're trimming the branches on a tree. Fewer, but stronger is the way to go.

Chapter 17

FIFTH DRAFT: FORMAT, SPELLING, AND GRAMMAR

You're almost there. This is the last draft in this whole process before you can consider your screenplay "done." Now, in reality, a screenplay isn't done until it has been made into a film and the film is in theaters. But, there is a point as a writer that you have to stop making changes. You are almost at that point. The last set of changes is technical, so the creative part of your brain can take a bit of rest on this last pass. Now you're going to focus only on the mechanical basics of your script: grammar, spelling, and screenplay format. Another open secret is most writers aren't great at these things. Who has time to learn all these rules when we're busy being creative, right? The real answer is that you don't have to be an expert but a working knowledge of these things can speed along the process of completing your script. It may sound a bit dry and academic, and it can be if you let it. The good news is, even with little skill in these fields, this is the fastest draft of the script. I can do a fifth draft in a few days. Thankfully, many modern technological advancements can help a lot. Be thankful for them.

I like to think of this draft as a final coat of wax on a beautiful car you've built from the ground up. You want your car/script to look its best, right? Of course you do! You wouldn't put a car in a showroom without waxing and polishing it, nor do you want someone to read your screenplay without (literally) crossing the t's and dotting the i's. With the amount of time you've spent on the script, you owe it to yourself and the script to make it look its best.

Grammar

There are plenty of grammar checking programs and websites that can catch and correct any mistakes. As of this writing, there are many free online grammar checkers. A few of them are writer.com/grammar-checker, www.grammarcheck.net/editor, and www.quillbot.com/grammar-check. These are helpful and will likely be enough to check any possible trouble areas in your script as you read through it. There is also the program that is currently growing in popularity called Grammarly. It has a free version and a paid version for $29.95/

month. This, and other programs like it, can be a good resource as well. Another option would be to hire a proper copy editor to take a look at your script. Sites like Upwork, Guru, and Creativepool can help with that. Most of the time, the free programs will be enough to get you through. But if you're especially unskilled at grammar and spelling or you are writing in a language that is not your first, these might be the way to go for you.

One item to note about these services, especially the free online ones: they aren't always right. These programs are often powered by some type of Artificial Intelligence that makes changes without human involvement. You should keep this in mind when using them. Sometimes they too make mistakes or suggest changes that aren't in line with what you want. Keep an eye on them. Don't just take everything they suggest as truth. If what they suggest doesn't feel right, don't change it.

Another thing to keep in mind with these programs is to preserve your style. What I mean is that you don't want to have these programs fix something that you meant to be incorrect on purpose. Mainly, this applies to dialogue. Often, characters and people in real life don't speak with perfect grammar. Depending on where someone is from, their education level, and their general attitude toward speech, they might speak very differently or poorly according to the established rules of grammar. Don't let an AI algorithm rob your characters of their unique way of speaking. These programs are merely there to make your script readable, not to make creative choices for you.

One last bit about grammar that can make it more difficult than spelling and format: your personal choice. The thing a grammar checker will never be able to catch is the way you want to write. When reading for grammar, you may simply want to change the wording of a sentence because you can simply come up with something better. It doesn't have to be a grammatically wrong sentence for you to dislike it. Many times in my writing, I find I can state something more concisely even if I got the grammar spot on. This is why grammar is more complex than the others. You still have room to make creative choices here, albeit pretty minor ones. That said, every choice you make in your screenplay matters. There is still a bit of room for improvement here when it comes to cutting out words or making sentences read more smoothly.

Spelling

When it comes to spelling, let's not complicate things. Use spell check. Every program has it. In Final Draft, it's under Tools. There's no algorithm that can misinterpret something. Either words are spelled correctly or not. There is no reason for your script to have any spelling errors. Use it, fix anything that needs fixing. That is all. Let's move on.

Format

Formatting is the final part of this draft. The reason I deal with it last is that it is usually the part of the script that needs the least amount of fixing. Whatever program you are using should be doing almost all of the formatting for you. With that said, it never hurts to run the formatting checker in your screenwriting program. In Final Draft, it is called Format Assistant and is again located under the Tools menu. Pay close attention to this as it runs. Sometimes, it can call an intentional choice an error. Most often, I run into it saying "an element should not be blank" when I intentionally left a line blank to break up the action. I just hit "ignore" and move on. Other than that one, it can be an extremely helpful tool to fix something you did during a draft and just didn't notice it.

Now that you've changed any awkward sentences, fixed any misspelled words, and your format is flawless. You know what that means, don't you? That's right...

YOU DID IT! YOUR SCREENPLAY IS COMPLETE! CONGRATULATIONS!

It's been a long, hard road. You've lived through the drama, humor, ups, downs, and everything in between. In some ways, writing a screenplay is as much a journey for you as it is for your characters. But now, more than ever, you can say you are a screenwriter. At this point, you have a professional, polished screenplay. No one can take that away from you. Well done. Reward yourself with a treat and rest easy. You've earned it.

Chapter 18

FEEDBACK

You've completed a polished draft of your screenplay. You've rewarded yourself and taken some time away from the script. Now what? It sounds scary, but now you have to let someone else read it. The reason for this is twofold. First, if you keep making changes and endlessly tinker with it, eventually you will change the entire core of the script. Before long, you will no longer recognize it. Often, you can change a script so much that you will no longer even like it. It can get to the point where it seems foreign to you. It will feel a million miles away from your original, pure idea. Trust me, you don't want that. Changes to your script hit a point of diminishing returns after a while. Secondly, without feedback, you are operating in a vacuum. When you are this deep into a screenplay, you have no objectivity. You might think you do, but you don't. You may think it's the worst screenplay of all time or you might think it's a masterpiece. Chances are it's somewhere in between. It's simply not possible to truly know if your script is any good without the involvement of others. This is why I like to call this draft the Reader Draft.

I should note that this step is entirely optional if you have no desire to pursue screenwriting professionally. If all you want is to have written a screenplay then you're done. You don't have to let anyone else read it. Writing a feature length screenplay is an accomplishment unto itself. If you've done it purely for your own fulfillment or simply to become a better writer, then more power to you. I'm happy to have helped. Feel free to skip to Chapter 19.

Getting Notes

Of course, the next question is, "Who do I get to read my script?" This is an important decision to make. There are a few steadfast rules I like to follow when it comes to getting my screenplay read. Number one on the list is don't let either of your parents or grandparents read it. This never helps. It only hurts. The main reason is they are biased. They love you. They can't help but like what you make. Showing them a screenplay is just the adult version of showing them a scribbled crayon drawing when you were a child. Even if it's garbage, they're still going to put it on the refrigerator. Also, they might get offended by it. The way you were raised can seep into your characters without you noticing. It's part of who you are and can't be helped. Then you let your father read it and have to explain to him why the father character in the script is an abusive alcoholic. Furthermore, your parents don't want to read something that they didn't expect could come from their child. This is especially true if you write a horror movie. How could their perfect little angel write about innocent people dying in disgusting, gory ways? Oh my! Avoid the parents and elders read. If you can manage it, don't let anyone who loves you read it. They are implicitly biased. What you want in a set of script notes more than anything is unbiased honesty. Loved ones, through no fault of their own, cannot provide that.

A second important component of letting others read your script is to get more than one person to do it. Ideally, you should get an odd number of people to read this draft. I like to get five or seven people to read mine. Why an odd number? Because if there is a similar note that is given by multiple readers, then you can weigh it against those who didn't give that note. For example, if you let five people read it and three of them hate the protagonist, that is a majority. And if four or more of those people all hate the protagonist, you should definitely address that issue. It's almost like a voting system. If there is a majority that gives the same note that means that you should take a hard look at it and consider making changes.

Find Your People

Another tip I have for feedback is to develop a community. This one can take time, but it's worth it. Do your best to assemble a solid core group of people who you can send your script to for honest feedback. In the best case scenario, these will be other writers. Exchanging your scripts with other screenwriters is the best way to get intelligent, applicable feedback. I have a great group of fellow writers who I know won't blow smoke up my backside when it comes to how good my script is. Most importantly, they know how to give thoughtful suggestions for changes that I can actually use. There is also mutual respect between writers. No one ever says, "Your script sucks! Throw it in the trash!" Other writers will understand that asking for feedback can be exposing and scary. They also know how much work a screenplay can be. This means they know how to critique without being hurtful.

How do you find these people? You'll likely meet other writers online these days. With social media, there are endless writers groups to join that are free of charge. I've met a variety of other writers on Instagram, some of which have become trusted givers of feedback. Also, there are writers groups in every city. Check out some Facebook groups, too. Other screenwriters are out there, you just have to look. If you've tried and failed to get a band of writer friends together, another option could be people whose creative opinions you trust. It could be a painter friend who has good taste, a photographer whose work you enjoy, a bookworm cousin who knows what a good story is, or simply someone who watches a ton of movies. Often, I find the opinion of a non-writer can be just as helpful as a professional writer's. After all, if your script ever becomes a film, you want people other than just screenwriters to go and see it. If all else fails you do have one more option: paid notes. There are plenty of feedback companies online that will read your script for a price. The main benefit of these groups is that the readers don't know you at all so the feedback is as unbiased and honest as possible. The drawback, of course, is that they cost money and can require some form of membership. I would say they are the last resort, but they can be useful. Talentville, Coverfly, Stage 32, and ScriptMother are just a few of the many companies that offer these services. If you're going to use one, be sure to research it first so you don't get scammed. Also, you'll want to register and copyright your script before sending it to anyone. We'll get to that later.

Asking for notes from someone is a delicate situation. It's a lot to ask of someone to read a 100+ page document and then provide written feedback on it. Most people don't want a homework assignment. With that in mind, it pays to be nice and offer something in return. If this is a fellow writer, I always offer to give them notes on anything they have to show me. This is a fair trade. If the person isn't a writer, this can be more complex. Now, I'm not telling you to bribe someone to read your script. You still want unbiased feedback. But, it never hurts to buy somebody lunch or send them a gift card as a way of saying thank you. Another thing is to give people time. Don't ask someone to read your script and then pester them to tell you what they thought. This can be hard when you've sent your script out and not heard back for weeks, or even months. Be patient. Be grateful. Just remember: everyone is busy these days. Give them ample time. Don't forget that they are doing you a favor.

What Notes To Use

You've sent your script out to several thoughtful, professional, and honest peers. Now you have a nice, fat crop of notes to go through. How do you separate the useful from the useless, the wheat from the chaff, the best from the worst? And how do you do it without crying over how terrible this will make you feel about your script? First things first: don't take it personally. I know this is easier said than done. Keep in mind that they are not attacking you. In fact, it's not an attack at all. It's a critique, a suggestion, an annoyance. This is not some personal insult to you as a human being. Even with as much time, effort, and thought you've put into your script, at this stage, you have to tell yourself it's just a screenplay. It's just a story. You're a writer, not an air traffic controller. No one is going to die here. It's just a note. Don't let it get to you. Another thing to bear in mind is that they are core notes and the people writing them are there to help you. They want your script to improve. Change is a good thing. Personally, I can't wait to hear what changes I should make. I welcome notes with open arms. I know my script isn't perfect. No script is. After so much time working on it, I need others to point out the imperfections. That's what notes are: ways to fix imperfections in your screenplay. If you built a house and forgot to put a door on it, the person that points this out doesn't hate your house. They are trying to help you. Let them.

Which notes should you integrate into your script and which should you disregard? For me, there are two types of notes that I use. First and foremost, there are the notes I mentioned before: ones that are the same recurring issue for multiple readers. If a majority of the readers come back with the same note, I absolutely examine that part of the script with absolute attention. More often than not, this causes me to fix that issue. The other notes I incorporate are the ones that improve my screenplay. Sometimes, you'll get notes that are simply a sideways move for the script. They don't hurt it, but they don't really help it either. There is no point in changing something that works just for the sake of being different. The notes that help the most are the ones that make you realize something you hadn't when writing. That something can be better. These are the notes that only come from an outside perspective. For example, I've had someone point out a plot hole that I didn't notice, but that then helped me sort out an entirely different part of the script that I wanted to change. A note that improves one part of the script can have a domino effect on other issues that need fixing.

Which notes do I disregard? That's an easy one: notes that don't fit into my vision for the story. If I receive a note that is well intentioned, but I feel is simply not right for my script, I don't use it. Keep in mind that the reader of the script is not able to read your mind. Only you truly know what you want to accomplish with your story. I've received notes in the past that were technically great improvements, but simply weren't in line with the tone I was going for, or weren't the direction I wanted to take a character, or I instinctively felt just didn't work. When evaluating a note, you have to ask yourself, "Does this make sense for the story I am trying to tell?" If not, don't use it. There is no rule stating you have to use a note from a reader. Even if it's a good one. Also, any reader worth their salt won't take any offense. As much as notes help, ultimately, it's your script and it's your decision.

Giving Notes

When asking for feedback on your screenplay, it's important to offer your feedback to other writers as well. A script swap can be hugely beneficial to both writers. After the notes are exchanged, discussing each other's scripts is one of the best ways to improve your screenplay. These exchanges have led to some of my best writing. With that in mind, how do you *give* a note? The first thing is not a note at all. Before reading someone else's script, I clarify what they want out of it. I ask if they only want creative notes or whether I should give them format, spelling, and grammar notes as well. Sometimes a writer plans to fix those things in a later draft and simply wants feedback on their story, not technical issues.

Next, I ask if they need it in a specific period of time. I don't offer feedback on a script if I know I don't have the time to give it the attention it deserves. Once I know what the writer wants to get out of our script swap, I read twice to make sure I have a full understanding of it. You can miss story or character points on the first read. Then I simply mark, either on paper or digitally, with a pen in the margins. I also include a summary at the end of what I liked and what I think can be improved. Notice I didn't say, "What I didn't like." Improvements are not hostile. They are helpful. The main thing about giving notes is that you want to be critical, but not hurtful. Giving your newborn screenplay to someone else is extremely difficult, especially for a first time writer. Be honest, but tread lightly. Start with the positive. Assure them that there were aspects of the script you liked. Be specific. If there isn't much to like, emphasize what little you did enjoy. As for issues, point out obvious things like plot holes, character mistakes, or parts you found confusing. I start these notes with phrases like, "I felt _____," "Did you mean_____?" "I wasn't sure about _____," "What if _____." For example, a note I could give would be: "When John ran back into the burning house, did you mean for him to save the cat? Because we see the cat later but it was in the house in that scene." The best notes to give also give a suggested change. Such as, "I think if you added John heroically carrying the cat from the burning building, that would be a great image." Notice how the notes are all from my perspective? I'm not telling the writer that these are absolute, carved-in-stone problems with their script. I'm simply letting them know what I *think* are issues. Keep in mind they gave you their screenplay for your reaction to it. The best notes keep things positive and helpful and even suggest an improvement.

When giving notes, there are a few things to avoid. Number one on the list is don't attack them personally. "You aren't good at writing scene descriptions," doesn't help anyone. Something like, "I think some scenes could use more clear descriptions," is gentler and about the script, not them. Also, keep notes actionable for the writer. "The villain is lame," is not something specific the writer can fix. "The villain feels like they could use more dimension. I would add a scene or two more of character development for them," is a clear-cut action they can take to make a change. Notes that are personal and not applicable to the craft of writing are not helpful.

Giving and getting notes on your screenplay can be an intimidating prospect. If you only write for yourself, you can save yourself the effort. That is completely valid for your journey as a writer and don't let anyone tell you otherwise. But if you plan on writing in a professional capacity, feedback is an absolutely vital part of the process. If you learn to not take notes personally and develop a thick skin you will be fine. Furthermore, gathering together a network of trusted peers for notes, script swaps, and discussions can be greatly helpful and fulfilling for any writer. Soon enough, you'll welcome notes when they come in. You'll see them for what they are: opportunities to make your script that much better.

Chapter 19

WRITING ROUTINE

Knowing the steps to write a screenplay is incredibly important, but they don't help much if you don't put them into action. You need a routine. You'll never finish in a timely way if you don't create one. Developing a process is the only way to crank through those pages draft after draft. The best way to get there is to use repeated steps when you're ready to write. You need to be in a clear and motivated mindset to write effectively. If you have a process or ritual you go through each time you write, after a while, you will naturally fall into "writer mode" when it's time to put words to paper. This is when the words come easily and ideas flow naturally. Once in this mindset, you are giving yourself the best chance to have a productive writing session.

Location

The first thing you'll need is a workspace that you feel comfortable in. Somewhere that you can concentrate on your ideas. For some, that's a quiet place at home. Others prefer a coffee shop. Wherever you feel most at ease is where you want to be. Just make sure it is free of distractions. There are few things worse for a writer than distractions. In today's world, there are plenty. Part of the reason I write my rough draft on paper instead of typing it is that I can't be distracted by all of the things you can do on a computer. No internet, no social media, and no excuses for not writing. I have to remove myself from that, so I go to a coffee shop without a computer for everything up to and including that rough draft. It is a place where there is only me and the paper. I *have* to write there because there isn't much else to do. When I sit down there, I am already in writer mode. So, you just have to find a place like that for you. As long as you can be alone with your ideas and distraction free you've found the right place.

The perfect view for a writing session

Set Goals

Next, you need to set a personal goal for each writing session. Make it something challenging, but attainable. Every writer would love to write 100 pages a day, but it's just not going to happen (unless you're some kind of prodigy). My goal is 10 pages a day. That works for me. For you, it could be five, fifteen, or more. I would suggest starting low and increasing once you know how much you're capable of. It can take some time to land on the right number. Having a set goal is important, but don't beat yourself up if you can't reach it sometimes. Some days my ten pages feel unreachable. On others, I leave ten pages in the dust. That is another point: you'll have days where your output isn't what you want. On other days, you will overperform. This is normal. For example, my personal record high for pages in a single writing session is 48. Do you know what my record low is? You guessed it...zero. The only truly consistent thing about being a writer is inconsistency. Get used to it. It's not a negative. It keeps things interesting. I don't know a single writer who hits the same page count every single day without fail. But that's why writing routines and goals exist in the first place. You're giving yourself a fighting chance.

Make Time

The next hurdle to clear is time. How long should you write each session? This is something else where you need to be consistent. Personally, three hours a day works for my life. Don't have that much time? That's perfectly okay. People have busy lives and setting aside time can be difficult. It is also helpful if that time is the same time of day. Again, this is a personal preference and may take time to settle into. I like to write from 2pm to 5pm. Whatever time of day or night you prefer will do. When you write doesn't matter, the actual writing is what counts. But, you must set some time aside for that writing if you want to finish your script. Even if that time is only fifteen minutes a day, after one month, you will have worked nearly eight hours on your script. I certainly recommend more than that if you can manage it, but any time spent writing your script is time making progress.

All progress is progress. A writing session doesn't always have to be putting out pages. Pages are the best thing to produce during a writing session, but they aren't the only thing. Some days, and they will happen, you won't write many pages. You won't hit your goal. This doesn't mean that your writing session is a waste. For example, if I've written two pages of garbage that I know I will rewrite or cut later, I will put away the script itself and work on some other aspect of it. Notice I didn't say I edit. Once again, never edit a rough draft until it is complete. Working on characters, research, or coming up with more scenes for your outline is still a writing session. There is no shame in admitting to yourself that the pages aren't coming. If you've set aside that time, use it. Working on your script in any way can be fulfilling. The routine is what will get you through when you're just not feeling up to it. All progress is progress.

Make It Personal

Make your writing routine as personal as possible. Tailor it to as many needs as you have. The point is to make yourself comfortable and relaxed enough to write without interruption. You don't have to use all of these tips. In fact, you don't have to use any of them. You can come up with your own set of ideas if you want. There are as many writing routines as there are writers. But, you must formulate a routine for yourself. David Lynch famously went to Bob's Big Boy diner every day for seven years. He'd order coffee and a milkshake at 2:30pm and work on his films. That's discipline. You don't have to go that far but it's the discipline of the routine that will get the work done. So, make it yours. Make it your own little ritual. Pick a brand of pens you like. Use a certain notebook for ideas. Go to the same location to write. Order the same coffee or lunch. Get a writer bag together and keep all of your appropriate materials in it. Get yourself some comfortable headphones to block out the world with music. Get whatever you need to relax.

Once you have all of these components working together, you can't help but feel like you have the tools to tackle any writing session. You're not going into battle with no ammo. You're locked and loaded. I start to feel myself slipping into a creative mindset as soon as I pick up my writer bag. You too will soon snap into "writer mode" with ease. You'll have a heap of confidence before you even put a word on the page. And that is the best a writer can ask for. This is how a writer can prepare themselves. This is what separates a productive writer from one that gives up and never finishes. This is how great writing gets done.

Chapter 20

SCREENWRITING MYTHS DEBUNKED

Screenwriting is now over 100 years old. That's a long time for something to be studied and practiced. Unfortunately, along with study and practice comes plenty of rumors, guesses, and myths. Many of these persist to this day. It now seems like what should merely be guidelines or advice has now become the intractable rules carved into stone tablets on Mount Screenplay. So, let's take a look at a few particularly questionable myths about screenwriting and see why they don't apply to real life writing.

1. **You have to write every day:** Let's tackle the big one first. I should start by saying that I do write every day. It works for me and I have the time to do it. I still miss a day here and there. Writing every day is helpful and you should do it if you can. But do you *have* to write every day? Absolutely not. I know plenty of well-paid professional writers who don't. We all have lives to lead outside of our writing sessions. If you're a first time writer, this is especially true. You are taking on a time consuming activity and fitting it into your existing daily schedule. This is compounded by day jobs, children, friends and family commitments, etc. Don't get upset with yourself, or let others get upset with you, if you can't write every day. Now, I'm not saying you should write ten words and then take a month off, but skipping a day here and there will not ruin your script. As I said earlier, all progress is progress. What will also help is the process of writing out all of your notes. With all of that information in hand, jogging your memory after not writing for a bit will be no problem at all. All of that said, one fascinating thing about becoming a writer is that soon you will *want* to write every day. Your script will start to have a magnet-like pull on you and you'll feel the need to write every day. It's an interesting feeling that I've come to love. When you get to that point, even writing a sentence on days you have no time can satisfy the need. When they said that you have to write every day, no one ever said how much.

2. **Your screenplay must have a three act structure:** This is categorically false. Completely untrue. The three act structure is only

so common because it is easily replicated. Most movies do have a simple beginning, middle, and end. They are what audiences expect and can easily process. Odds are, your screenplay will fall neatly into that space. But, there is nothing wrong with writing something more or less complex. Many successful films have no identifiable act structure. For example, the films of Jim Jarmusch, David Lynch, or Richard Linklater. These can sometimes be called "slice of life" films. These films are more about exploring settings and characters but have little in the way of plot. In short, the characters in these films simply "hang out." There are also plenty of films with more than three acts. Examples include *Sicario (2015)*, *The Girl with the Dragon Tattoo (2011)*, and *Run Lola Run (1998)*. Each of these films has a five act construction, closer to a stage play. A five act script utilizes a prologue or first act that sets up the world and covers character backgrounds/exposition. Acts Two and Three set up and intensify the conflict. After this, Act Four is a resolution while Act Five looks to the future. This ending is sometimes called the Tag or Dénouement (if you want to get pretentious about it). So, if you have a bigger or smaller idea for your script that doesn't fall into the traditional three act structure, you don't need to change it just so it fits in that box. Three acts are nice and they are sometimes easier, but they aren't the only game in town.

3. **Your characters have to be likable:** You'll hear this word a lot while on your writing journey. If you're talking about the box office then, yes, your characters should be likable. If you're trying to write the next Hollywood blockbuster, go ahead and make your characters the most likable people on the planet. Look at the Avengers films. They have insanely likable characters (and tons to choose from). They also made money like they have their own printing press. That is fine and it's one way of writing your characters. But, if that's not your thing, your goal should be to make your audience *understand* your character. The audience doesn't have to like them,

they just have to grasp their motivations. The audience simply has to understand *why* they do what they do. They don't even have to agree with it on principle. Let's look at a classic example: Daniel Plainview from *There Will Be Blood (2007)*. By all accounts, this is a horrible person. He lies, manipulates, swindles, and abuses nearly everyone he comes into contact with. He is decidedly not likable. His motivations, however, are incredibly clear: he is willing to sacrifice everything for wealth. Not only are his motives clear, the audience doesn't, and shouldn't, agree with him. Part of the reason he is interesting is that he is so different from what the audience can relate to. But they understand it. You'll hear that a more likable character is a more successful character. It's a better character. This depends on what kind of movie you are writing. If you plan on writing broadly appealing family films or crowd-pleasers, you should make your protagonist likable. There is nothing wrong with that. And if successful, you'll have plenty of box office gold to prove it. If you're writing just for yourself, or plan on something of a more specific genre, then your characters can be as unlikable as you see fit. Just make the audience understand them.

4. **Your first draft is good enough because of your God-given talent:** Way too many first time writers have convinced themselves that they are supernaturally gifted. They think that their first draft is perfect and that rewriting is for suckers. They act like this because they think they are so naturally talented that they don't need to do more than one draft. They are wrong. The real reason they don't write more drafts is that they are egotistical and they are afraid. Being a professional writer of any kind means opening yourself up for rejection. This isn't to be negative, this is just a fact. If you present your work professionally, it can be rejected. That is what these writers truly fear. You can't present your writing to any professional outlets without having rewritten it first. This means, in theory, if you never rewrite your script, it will never be rejected. The whole "I'm so talented I don't need to rewrite" men-

tality is merely a defense mechanism. Many screenwriters, myself included, would love it if rewrites weren't part of the process. But they are an integral part. Your first draft may be fine. Sometimes I like mine. But never tell yourself that it is flawless. It's not. Don't lie to yourself. A big part of being a writer is being honest with yourself and your readers. And, honestly, you need a rewrite (or four). Now, I'm not saying God-given talent doesn't exist. It most certainly does. I know plenty of talented people. Many of them are more talented than me. But, the difference is that the work I put in allows me to finish what I start. The routine, the rewriting, the long hours; this is what gets your writing done. Talent is the easy part. You don't have to work for talent. You either have it or you don't. What gets it done is refining and shaping your script until you have something professional. A finished commodity that you can show anyone and be proud of. That's what rewriting gets you.

5. **Your idea will be stolen:** Speaking of showing others your work, don't hesitate to do so. Many beginning writers feel that their precious idea will be snatched away by some Hollywood bigwig and they'll be left penniless. This is highly unlikely. I'm not saying it's never happened, but it is exceedingly rare. The odds of getting in a room to pitch to someone with such power are low to begin with. Then they decide to cut you out and steal your idea? That's another set of low odds. The reality is that someone with enough power to steal your idea and make the film themselves would not have gotten that much power by screwing over writers. Does that make sense? Why would they risk their entire reputation in the business to save themselves your screenwriter's fee? They wouldn't unless they are exceedingly careless and stupid. I'm not saying these careless and stupid types don't exist, but there aren't enough to worry about. Furthermore, just being able to pitch your script to these kinds of folks is rare. This is your first script so the odds are unlikely that you'll even have to worry about them. I'm also not encouraging you to actively give away your ideas to shady producers

or other writers. Use your best judgment. If you feel like you don't want to tell someone your idea, don't. It's your intellectual property. I'll pitch my idea to almost anyone, that's why I memorize the loglines for my screenplays. Beyond that, if somebody asks, I've got a perfect three to five sentence mini-pitch ready to go. Without knowing it, you could be pitching to a person who can buy your script and make your movie happen. Another big reason I don't worry about idea theft is that I copyright all my screenplays and register them with The Writers Guild of America (WGA). It's an inexpensive and easy process we'll get into the details of later. Knowing I've got legal proof of my ideas and when I wrote them gives me great peace of mind when pitching my ideas. This will help you, too. Don't be afraid to share your creativity with others.

6. **You must write a script for a certain market:** One of the worst things a creative person can do is chase trends and markets. The whole point of writing a screenplay, painting a picture, recording a song, etc. should be because you need to do it. You want to do it. It is what is fulfilling to you. As much as we say otherwise, deep down, art is for the artist. Yes, we want our screenplays to become movies. Yes, we want to make money. Yes, we want others to enjoy what we make. But that's not the original reason we do it. Who we don't write for is marketers. People who tell you what others want at the moment. Those people will tell you who will like your screenplay if you just change x, y, and z. Writing a screenplay is difficult enough. What you shouldn't burden yourself with further is the moving target of what is trendy. That is a losing game. Also, scripts can take a long time to write and then much longer to gain any industry traction (if that's what you're seeking). For example, you write a script about a political leader that will only be relevant while they are in office. By the time you finish the script, get feedback, pitch it to the right people, and the movie gets made, that political figure will likely be long gone from the national stage. And you will have wasted your life on a useless screenplay about

someone no one cares about. So, write something that is first and foremost for yourself. There is no other way to maintain your artistic integrity. Chasing the market or specific demographics is a fruitless endeavor.

7. **Formatting rules don't matter:** Many writers feel like the subject and substance of their screenplay should be what matters over all else and they can disregard the rules of formatting. The essence and meaning of the script are important, but not if they don't come across clearly. Formatting is merely a standardized way to ensure that a screenplay can be understood. Story, characters, and action are all valuable and formatting makes sure the reader can grasp them. In a professional sense, formatting also serves as a way of vetting writers. An agent, producer, or production company that reads screenplays has to know that a writer can be trusted to follow a simple set of rules. After all, they have to work with this writer if they like the script. But who wants to work with a writer who can't be bothered to follow a simple set of instructions? A set of instructions that a formatting program does most of the work on, no less. As mentioned earlier, Courier in 12 point is the standard font because every letter takes up the same space on the page. This is to ensure that all scripts maintain the same lengths. The other, little-known, reason for this is that professional screenplay readers for companies get paid by the script. So, if your format is all wrong if and when it gets into their hands, you could be costing them money. Not the first impression you want to make. These days it's not too hard to avoid these mistakes. The simple fact is formatting matters.

8. **Formatting must be flawless:** Formatting matters to the extent that it helps your script become comprehensible. As long as your formatting is mostly spot on, your story and characters will come through. What can end up hurting your script is when you worry more about format than your story and characters. If you forget a dash in a scene heading or there is a single typo in the script, no

one is going to throw it in the trash. As long as the script is good, that is. When it comes to making sure everything is presentable, it can become just like doing too many drafts. At a certain point, you hit diminishing returns. Just do your best, and if you aren't sure about something, read other scripts to see how they handled it, ask another writer for help, or simply cut it. As long as your formatting is consistent, looks clean, and conveys your ideas clearly, you've done your duty.

9. **Your idea must be original:** This one can be stressful. I know many writers who don't write enough simply because they are paralyzed by their lack of ideas. They don't realize that the way you write a movie can be original in itself. If you're a hardworking, talented screenwriter, the subject matter shouldn't matter. Or at least not matter enough to prevent you from writing. If you can't come up with something mind-blowing, simply pick something you're interested in and write your movie about that. Think of the types of films you like and then ask how they haven't yet been done. How you construct an idea for a screenplay is as important as the idea itself. Originality be damned. There have been many theories over the years that there are only six stories in human history anyway. That's not a lot. Even if that is true, screenplays get written and made into movies every day. Some of the best films in history aren't very original ideas. *The Godfather?* It's a gangster movie. *The Shawshank Redemption?* A prison break film. *Star Wars?* It's a space opera. Even before those movies, all of those genres had been done to death. That didn't stop them and the other great films from getting made. And it shouldn't stop you either. So, get over the thought that you can't write something because your idea isn't Earth-shattering. It won't be and doesn't have to be. You should never let that stop you from writing your script. If you do, you'll be frozen with doubt while others simply roll up their sleeves and get to work.

These myths are just a portion of what you'll hear in the screen-writing sphere. The main point is to take every bit of screenwriting customs with a healthy bit of skepticism. The history of screenwriting has produced a huge amount of information about the craft. Much of this is merely a guideline, speculation, or codified practices that don't broadly apply. Don't be fooled by what is supposedly set in stone. Don't let these ideas throw you off course. Don't buy into what doesn't work for you. Do what makes sense for you and your story. You are in charge.

Chapter 21

FINDING YOUR VOICE

ndividuality in writing is important. Notice I didn't say originality. That comes and goes, but your individual voice as a screenwriter is what makes you stand out. If you can hone your ability to make your script distinct then you have a huge leg up in this game. A writer who has a singular approach doesn't need originality. They can tackle any idea and the way they do it will set it apart from the rest. How do you put your stamp on something? How do you express your individuality? How do you find your voice?

You Are Unique

The first thing you have to identify is what makes you distinct as a person. This can be your personality traits, experiences, where you live, what you do or have done for a living, your family and friends, or any number of other topics. Maybe you're the first person in your family to go to college, climb a mountain, or learn a different language. Perhaps you were a roadie for the Rolling Stones in the 90s, witnessed the fall of the Berlin Wall, or rode a bronco in a rodeo. The point is, no matter who you are, there is something unique and interesting about your life. Even if you can't think of something, ask those around you. The answers you get may surprise you. Whatever it is about yourself you choose to focus on, that is your angle. That is your story.

The more personal your writing is, the better it is. Once you have your perspective, you have to approach it from your point of view. How do you want to portray the events of your script? What images or words come into your mind when you picture the film? This is what you should write down. Write truthfully from your heart and mind. Be completely honest with yourself. Don't alter what you know deep down should be on the page. Don't soften it. Don't make it digestible. Don't worry about what others will think. Moreover, don't try to emulate someone else. They aren't you. You are here to mine yourself for ideas. How you see things will set you apart.

Watch Everything, Read Everything, Question Everything

Another way to hone your voice is to watch your favorite films and read books. Then ask yourself, "What if?" What if the supporting character was the main character? What if the main character had parents like mine growing up? What if instead of the movie's location the events took place in my hometown? What would someone like me do in this situation? Bringing your personal perspective to an idea is what can make it unique. The reverse is also true. What if something in your own life had a plot twist? What if, instead of going to college, you moved to Europe and got recruited into a spy organization? What if when you were eight and rode your bike into the woods there was a crashed spaceship there? What if when you went on vacation you ran into your prom date and you fell back in love? Taking something personal and injecting a bit of excitement is another way to bring your perspective to a story.

Whatever you write should have meaning to you. Writing a screenplay is a time-consuming, labor intensive process. You have to stay motivated and having a personal meaning or reason for writing will keep you going. Whether you're exploring a subject that interests you, working through your personal feelings, or paying tribute to your favorite movie genre, it has to mean something to you on a deep level. If your script has significant meaning for you, chances are that will be apparent to a reader or audience. Hopefully, in turn, it will have meaning for them as well. This can be something you share with others if you want to, but I recommend keeping it a secret. I love this feeling. It's like being in a secret club with only one member. And that club's sole purpose is to write your screenplay. Writing something only for yourself is the purest form of writing because you aren't seeking validation from others. It's just yours. That has its own exclusive power and meaning. It can be freeing. That meaning and reasoning for writing your script is something you should define for yourself early and hold on to. Why you write is almost as important as what you write. Know it. Keep it. Protect it.

Gaining Self-confidence

As a writer, you'll need at least a bit of self-confidence. Often, screenwriters and movie fans can be introverts. Believe me, I am the biggest introvert you'll ever find. If that's the case, gaining confidence—especially in your work early on—can be daunting. But you need confidence to keep motivated and finish your work. Sometimes, it can be difficult to see your early writing as anything but subpar. I assure you, it's not as bad as you think it is. For me, four things helped change my mindset when I needed to feel better about my work:

1. **Don't ever speak badly about your work to others.** If someone asks, "Is your script any good?" your response 100% of the time should be, "Yes." You need to seem excited about your script, even if you aren't. This will not only convince others that your work is good, but will also impress upon them that you are confident and capable. If you keep this up, you will soon have an army of people who think you are a skillful writer, even if you feel that you aren't. But you know what a large group of people believing in you can do? It will cause you to *actually* believe in yourself. It can take a while, but it works. Nowadays, I don't have to fake any excitement when someone asks about my script. I am genuinely full of enthusiasm. You can hate your script as much as you want privately, but never speak ill of it to others.

2. **Call yourself a writer.** I didn't like calling myself a writer until I had written about five screenplays. I felt there was some sort of unspoken minimum standard to meet. There isn't. A solid measure of this is simply having something to show others. If you've finished a draft you like, go ahead and call yourself a writer. That way, you can at least have something to show off if you want to. You never know when you'll run into someone hungry to finance a film, so it helps to have something to feed them. This will also

feed your confidence. Don't say you're "dabbling" or "messing around." In the words of a famous Jedi, "Do or do not. There is no try." You're a writer now. Own it. It will help you feel better about everything you write going forward. This is because it won't be written by someone with no confidence, it will be written by a writer.

3. **Forget about Imposter Syndrome.** If you're unfamiliar, imposter syndrome is "the persistent inability to believe that one's success is deserved or has been legitimately achieved as a result of one's own efforts or skills." In other words, you've somehow tricked everyone into thinking you deserve something you don't. This ties in directly to calling yourself a writer. It's all about giving yourself permission to feel good about your work and yourself. You should. You deserve to. You earn it with every page, sentence, and word of your script that you write. Besides, there are no "writer police" who are going to kick down your door and demand you provide evidence that you are, in fact, a writer. You are one. Accept it and move on. There is nothing to feel bad about.

4. **Don't compare yourself to others.** This can be easier said than done. There will be times in your writing journey when you'll read about some virtuoso who wrote a screenplay in their crib at daycare and it's now going to be a 100 million dollar Hollywood epic. This might be an exaggeration, but stories like this can make you feel bad about your progress. Don't. Your progress is exactly that, *yours*. As I've mentioned, each writer is on their own journey. That journey is a different length for everyone. Some people have ten hours a day to write, others have fifteen minutes. That's just how life works. Your success or lack thereof is not a measure of the quality of your work. It is simply a matter of timing. Some will achieve success early, but the vast majority of writers achieve success later. Don't get discouraged by others' success. Just keep writing. As I have mentioned, any progress is progress. To further my point, here are some successful screenwriters who broke

out later in life: David Seidler (Oscar Winner for *The King's Speech* at age 74), Courtney Hunt (Oscar Nominated for *Frozen River* at age 44), Julian Fellowes (Oscar Winner for *Gosford Park* at age 53), Guillermo Arriaga (Oscar Nominated for *Babel* at age 49). There is no time limit for success.

Define Your Style

On a practical level, it also helps to define what writing style you will use. I touched on this point earlier. You should decide if your style will be workman-like or novelistic in approach. Will your writing be more for the reader or for the filmmakers bringing it to life later? I lean toward novelistic because I want the act of reading my screenplay to be a form of entertainment in itself. I want my reader to be able to picture the movie before it is made. Whereas a more workman-like script is for the filmmaking team. It allows the reader to know what the production will need in a more direct, uncluttered way. I recommend trying each style out for yourself and seeing what feels like a good fit for you. Another way to find out is to read screenplays or novels that are akin to these styles (Hemingway vs. Shakespeare, for example). Having a good idea in your head of how you are going to stylistically approach your writing will improve your personal expression.

Finding your voice can take time. Don't rush it or compare it to others. Be brave enough to try and fail at various styles until you find something that works for you. Remember, the more personal you can make your screenwriting, the better. Once you start bringing what makes you unique into your writing, that's when your style will take shape. Confidence in who you are as a writer is hugely important. Calling yourself a writer, forgetting about imposter syndrome, and speaking well of your work can help with that. Once you gain confidence, your voice and style will become even stronger. Who you are as an individual is one of the most valuable assets you have as a screenwriter. Don't waste it trying to emulate others. Your purpose for writing is what counts. Hold on to it. Use it.

Chapter 22

RESEARCH

Often neglected but crucially important, research is something you should do for your first script and all those that come after. Research can grant your script a bedrock of legitimacy that is absent from others' writing. While some may argue that research isn't strictly necessary for some stories, I would argue that there is always a small amount that needs to be done. At the other end of the spectrum, there may be a huge amount needed. Whether writers want to admit it or not, research can be a great help to any screenplay.

At this point, you're likely saying to yourself, "But, my script isn't based on a true story. It's also not a period piece." This is understandable. I've been there. It's one of the misconceptions that first time screenwriters can have. You've been programmed to believe those are the only types of films that need research. This is untrue. The fact is those are the only types that require *extensive* research. But what if you're writing something completely imaginary, like a science fiction or fantasy film? Isn't everything in those made up? Those don't need research, do they? I hate to be the one to break it to you, but yes, those need research too. There might be screenplays that required no research, but I haven't heard of any.

Period pieces require a hefty amount of research. Most of the time, extensive internet searching can help you nail down the appropriate clothing, technology, historical events, and way of speaking for a given time period. This is not necessarily difficult work, but it can take time. For example, if you're writing about police in Chicago in the 1970s, you'll need to find pictures of their uniforms, what make and model their squad cars were, what guns they were issued, etc. That's a lot of information. All of which is readily available online, but time consuming to gather. Once you have all that vital information, put it in your notes. Make sure it gets into the script. These are details that you want to get right if your goal is factual correctness. You don't want your script to be dismissed because it's supposed to take place at a specific time and place and you don't get anything right about that time and place. It looks unprofessional and lazy.

When it comes to true story screenplays, the importance of research is even greater. As discussed in Chapter 3, writing a true story requires life rights and all sorts of legal permissions. Assuming you have all that cleared, then you have to dig into the person's life. This is an enormous amount of work but can be made easier if the person is still alive or has lots of information published about them. Getting the details right about the events of a person's life is no longer an option, it's a responsibility. That said, it is highly unlikely that your first script will be a true story based on someone's life (unless you know them personally). Just be aware that period pieces and true stories are not the only types of screenplays that require research. They are the type that requires the most.

Why do the other types of screenplays also require research? The short answer is realism. Odds are, no matter what type of film you are writing, there are going to be details that you need to learn about. One example is characters with a specialty skill or job. Is your character a firefighter? You should learn about what their day-to-day work is like. This includes their education requirements, training, special skills, equipment, typical working day activities, schedule, and how it affects their personal lives. These are good things to know about any main character's job, even if it is not considered "skilled labor." Let's say you're writing a workplace comedy. Your protagonist works at a fast food burger joint. You should know how frying up burgers works. Also, how do they make a milkshake? Do they work long hours or just part-time? These details may seem insignificant but let's ask a question: which workplace comedy is going to be a better script, the one where the writer knows this information or the one where the writer just winged it and guessed? Odds are the researched script is going to be more authentic, will have more for the writer to mine for material, and will be more successful. Now, think if the character's job is something more complex. Let's say you're writing a sci-fi script that takes place in outer space. Researching space travel will help you immensely. Knowing how astronauts get to space and what they do when they get there can be endlessly fascinating to you and your audience. The writer knowing how all of it works is not only necessary but can be captivating for audiences. Having a good working knowledge of the main activity that your protagonist will be engaging in throughout the story is essential.

Gathering information on the internet or from books is merely one form of research. There are many ways to lend your screenplay authenticity or entertainment value through research. One of the best is to simply watch movies that are in the same genre as the one you are writing. First of all, this will help you come up with ideas. Remember asking "What if?" that can work here as well. I often get story ideas by seeing what has already been done in films and then thinking about how it could be different. Writing a bank heist film? Look up some of the best ones and watch a fistful. Then you can see how they handle the story and come up with something fresh and new. This also helps you learn the rules of the genre you are diving into. And then you can creatively break those rules. Does every bank heist movie you watch have a planning scene? Do you need one in your film? How can yours stand out from the rest? These are all questions you can ask and answer by watching films and taking notes. Another benefit is that you can find out what's already been done so you don't copy another film. And, of course, you also get to watch a bunch of great films under the guise of research. Learning has never been so fun. It doesn't always have to be movies either. Reading novels, watching interviews, or reading articles are also totally viable options. Research for your script doesn't always have to be cold, academic fact-finding.

How much research should you do? That is a question with many answers. I think it depends on the screenplay. As mentioned before, period pieces or true story scripts are known to require more research. But with any script, you have to stop at some point and start actually writing. I like to weigh how much I've learned about a subject against what I'm planning on putting in the story. Going back to the firefighter example, I would think about how much actual firefighting is taking place in my script. If the whole movie takes place in a fire station and at burning buildings, I know I need to do a lot of research. If my protagonist is a firefighter but the story is about their home life and their family relationships, perhaps I don't need to know what a Bresnan Cellar Nozzle is (FYI: it's a rotating nozzle tip that sprays water in a circular pattern.). The focus of the story should dictate the amount of research you do. Once you have a solid working knowledge of the subjects required for your screenplay, you should be ready to write your story. A good test is to think if someone asked you questions about your subject, would you be able to answer them with the information you've gathered? If the answer is yes, then your research is done. And if something pops up once you're further into your writing, you can always pause and search up the information needed to continue.

Research can also help you plan your style choices. As the old saying goes, "You have to know the rules to break them." That holds true here if you plan on diverging from the established rules of a genre. The most common form of this is deliberate historical inaccuracy. Let's say you're writing a film about the building of the pyramids in Egypt. In the modern day, it's an accepted historical fact that they were built by the Egyptian people. But in your script, they were actually built by space aliens. To accurately portray the building of the pyramids, you would need to do your research to gain that knowledge. Then in your script, you would have the freedom to subvert that by fleshing out how the aliens did it. You need to learn about something before you can present an alternate or fictional version. This is often done with anachronistic music in period pieces as well. An example of this is *Marie Antoinette (2006)* which is set in 1770 but is full of 1980s New Wave music. It works wonderfully. This kind of bold stylistic choice can only be done with the confidence of having done the research and then intentionally disregarding it. Note: these techniques are for *intentionally* making errors in historical fact or including anachronisms. This is not a license to simply ignore all facts merely to avoid putting in work with research.

Learning the clichés and tropes of a genre can also allow you to defy them with maximum impact. In many situations, this means doing the exact opposite of the established rules. This can help subvert audience expectations. Let's go back to the bank heist example. You've written a meticulous heist planning scene and you know that in that genre of film the heist gets pulled off right afterward. But what if it went instantly wrong and all your bank robbers are killed? Or the police bust in and the heist never happens at all? These are ways you can upturn the genre in which you are working. It can be a fresh angle to attack the story from. But, to do this, you must know the expectations within that genre. That comes from research.

Research can benefit your screenplay in plenty of ways. Much like character histories, at times it can get tiresome, but it pays off many times over in the end. It can inform characters, help with style, add realism, help you learn the rules of the genre, grant your script legitimacy, and make it more impactful. That's a slew of advantages you can give yourself over someone who neglects research. On top of all that, it can be fun. One of the great things about writing a screenplay is the ability to live and learn through your characters. You can learn about people you would like to meet and answer questions you've always wondered about. You can investigate subjects you have always been interested in. Learning about something or someone you never knew existed is interesting. Then you get to use all of that newfound information to strengthen your screenplay. If your script is a house, think of research as the concrete foundation on which to build. You need to feel confident that it can handle the weight of your story. Much like character histories or negative feedback, research is not something to be dreaded or feared. It is yet another opportunity to improve your screenplay. And when it comes to writing your first script, you'll want to take all of those opportunities you can.

| Chapter 23 |

COPYRIGHTS & CONTESTS

You've come a long way. The screenplay you've crafted is now as polished as it can be. It is as close to finished as you can get it. Now what? If you so choose, it's time to release it out into the world and see how it is received. One quick and easy way of doing that is entering it into screenplay contests. But first, you need to make sure it is protected. You've spent enough time on your baby that you don't want to drive it around without a car seat. So you need to register it with The Writers Guild of America and copyright it with The U.S. Copyright Office. If you plan on showing anyone else your script, entering contests is optional, registration and copyrighting it is not.

Writer's Guild Registration & Copyright

Let's start with the easy one: Writers Guild of America (WGA) registration. The WGA is the writers' union in Hollywood. Don't worry, you don't have to be a member to register your script with them. You don't have to live in America, either. But if you do and you live West of the Mississippi River, you'll want to register with WGAW (West). If you live East of it, then you'll register with WGAE (East). It's quite easy. Simply go to the website. West is www.wgawregistry.org/ and East is www.wgaeast.org/mo/script_registration/registrations. As of this writing, it's only $25 and is well worth it. Simply fill out the form, pay, and upload your script file. It should be in PDF format. To save your script as a PDF in Final Draft go to "File→Save As PDF." Registration lasts for a period of five years. While it does not technically establish ownership, WGA registration establishes *when* the script was written and is admissible in court should someone ever steal your work. Before you register make sure your script is completely finished as you will not be able to make changes to it once it is registered. If you change it later, you must re-register the new version. One perk is they send you a nice certificate (pictured). Put this in a frame and show it to anyone who ever doubted that you are a real writer.

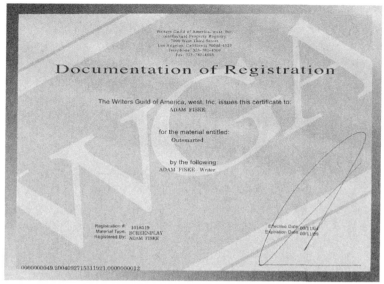

The WGA Certificate for my first screenplay

Now the tricky one: copyright. I'm not going to lie to you, this one is a bit annoying (dealing with the US government, am I right?). Go to www.copyright.gov/registration/performing-arts/. You have to set up an account and fill out the form. It's much longer, has a number of steps, and is more tedious. After that, you pay the fee, which is $35-$65 at the time of this writing. I suggest using the digital file upload option. It's cheaper and you don't have to mail in a physical copy of your script. Again, you'll have to submit a PDF of your script. Make sure the script is fully polished and needs no more changes. This time, there is no cool certificate, it's merely a confirmation email or a letter in the mail. The processing also takes longer. They say it can take from one month to a year to process. I've personally never had it take more than four months to receive confirmation. The upside of this more involved process is the protection you receive is much more substantial. The main reason to copyright a screenplay is that you can file a "copyright infringement" lawsuit if your idea is stolen. Copyright acts as proof of ownership. You own the rights to the written copy, hence the name copyright. This means you own the ideas expressed in your script. This is a much bigger deal than WGA registration. Essentially, copyright allows you to take legal action about ownership and recoup legal fees and damages if you win your case in court. I'm not a lawyer and have not had my script stolen so that is the extent of my knowledge. Just think of WGA registration as the time stamp of your writing with less legal muscle behind it. Think of copyright as ownership with legal action available. Copyright law is a complex issue and other resources cover it better than I can in this chapter. As a screenwriter, I would say you should register with the WGA regardless. If you plan on presenting your screenplay professionally to contests, agents, managers, and production companies, it is a good idea to copyright the script as well. Remember, anyone that is professional will not look at your script without at least one of these protections in place.

Screenplay Contests

Speaking of contests, let's take a look at how they can help you. If you're like the vast majority of writers, you don't have an agent or manager. This is not the only way to drum up some industry interest in your screenplay or, at the very least, get some feedback. One way to get your toe in the water without representation is through screenplay contests. For new writers, they can be a great opportunity to put their script out in the world. Many contests offer feedback and notes which can be very helpful to new writers, especially if you are having difficulties getting meaningful feedback from those you know. This feedback can cost extra, but it is usually from an established professional. This means the notes can actually be helpful. I find the extra money is worth it if the contest is reputable and you're sick of hearing friends and family simply say, "It was pretty good." If you win something in any contest, you're now an "award-winning screenwriter." Congratulations! Another unsung benefit of these competitions is they force you to deal with rejection with fewer consequences. You won't get selected for every contest you enter. If you get into half of them, you're doing great. So when your script isn't selected, it's not the end of your career, but it does allow you to get used to a certain level of failure. Part of writing is rejection; it's just how it works. Getting rejected by a low stakes script contest hurts, but it hurts a lot less than getting tossed out of the office of a high powered production executive.

How do you enter? Right now, the best way is to get yourself an account on Filmfreeway.com. This is basically a film contest shopping website. Make an account, upload your WGA registered PDF of your script and start browsing. The major convenience here is you can look up a ton of contests and add them to a cart and pay all the entry fees at once. You don't have to track down each contest's website and fill out an entry form each time. It's a hugely helpful service and I can't recommend it enough for beginners or seasoned writers. They also allow users to review their contest experience, so you can feel secure in knowing what kind of contest it is and if it's right for your script. That said, a few of the most prestigious contests are not listed on the site, so you still have to track them down and enter each one.

Note: never enter a screenwriting contest you haven't researched. You never know if someone is running a scam. This is why you should use sites like FilmFreeway, so there is a middleman or buffer.

Which contests should you enter? In my experience, contests often fall into two categories: 1. The industry-leading highly esteemed contests that are extremely competitive & cost a pretty penny to enter. 2. The lesser known, less competitive contests that also cost much less to enter. The plain truth is that there aren't too many of the first variety because those can offer real world career opportunities for the winners. This is why they receive thousands of entries each year and are exceedingly difficult to win or place in. There are plenty of the second kind. Almost every screenplay contest will promise "industry connections" and "exposure." Most of the time, this isn't exactly the truth. They often overpromise. You can't really blame a small contest for wanting to get bigger by having an overblown sales pitch. Now, this doesn't mean you shouldn't enter these contests. Quite the opposite. Since these contests have far fewer entries than their big industry counterparts, there is a much higher chance of you doing well in the competition. Also, they're a lot cheaper to enter. While a silver prize from Reelz R' Us Screenwriting Contest isn't the same as an Oscar, it's still a win. For a new writer, that can give your confidence a big boost. Also, you get a cool laurel with wheat around it and share it with everyone you know. Some also have trophies. If your script is good and you enter enough of these contests, you have the chance to rack up some accolades. With either kind of contest, you should pay extra for feedback if you can afford it. Helpful notes can come from anywhere. I've received good notes from contests that cost anywhere from $15 to $150 to enter. Good feedback is good feedback.

If you know what you want out of a contest going in, you won't be disappointed. For the prestigious contests, know that it is unlikely you will place or win, but even entering can carry a sense of accomplishment. In addition, their feedback is usually great. And you could win or place, you never know. It's worth a shot if you have the money to enter. As I like to say, you can't hit a homerun without taking a big swing. With the smaller, lesser-known contests, there's a much higher chance of winning an award or placing, but don't go in thinking that Hollywood will be blowing up your phone.

Let's take a look at some of the most famous contests. You should enter at least one of these if you have the money:

1. **Academy Nicholl Fellowship** - Yes, *The* Academy. This contest is put on by the same folks that hand out The Oscars every year. Placing in the Top 10 in this contest will get you noticed by some major players in the industry. Hugely competitive. 7,000+ people enter every year. Grand Prize: $35,000.

2. **ScreenCraft** - This is a very well respected organization. I encourage you to check out the website even if you don't enter the contest. Lots of categories to win, so no matter what genre script you have, there will be a place to enter. They also offer the ScreenCraft

Fellowship. Lots of past winners have signed with agents and managers and have worked for major studios. Grand Prize: $1,000.

3. **BlueCat Screenplay Competition** – A notoriously tough, but rewarding contest. A big bonus is you get professional feedback without any extra cost. Aaron Guzikowski (*Prisoners, Raised by Wolves*) placed in the finals in 2005. There are many other success stories as well. Grand Prize: $5,000.

4. **Austin Film Festival Screenplay Competition** - This is an excellent contest for those who want something more valuable than just cash. If you place in this contest, you get to network at The Austin Film Festival. You get invited to discussions, workshops, and more. A festival experience is worth its weight in gold. It also has plenty of different categories and prizes.

5. **Final Draft Big Break Contest** - Put on by the very software we use to write. This is a good contest if you want to meet with agents and managers. The judges many times *are* agents and managers. Plenty of success stories. Winning and placing gets you a slew of industry meetings. Grand Prize: $10,000.

For the smaller contests, I would say to simply check out FilmFreeway. You can sort the contests in several ways (including the price of entry), which can help you figure out the right contests for you. If you're not sure, enter a few of the inexpensive ones at first to get a feel for the contest experience.

Overall, I recommend putting your script into a few contests once it's finished, registered with The WGA, and copyrighted. They can help you grow as a writer with feedback, win you an award or two, or even get your foot in the door of the industry. If and when you get rejected, you can use this as an opportunity to grow. Every time I've gotten a rejection notice, I like to think of it like this: I can cross them off the list of potential supporters. I don't think of it as a rejection, I think of it as a filtering out process. They might not have loved your script, but now you can focus on fewer contests. That means less work for you. That's called turning a negative into a positive. A useful skill in the screenwriting field. On the other hand, if you win anything, it will be a huge boost in your confidence. If you set realistic expectations and treat them as a chance to hone your craft, rather than your ticket to the big time, screenwriting contests can be a valuable avenue for any new screenwriter.

Chapter 24

YOU MADE IT!

Y ou did it. You're here. It's the end of your first journey into screen-writing. You have come further than most. What you have achieved is not an easy task. You are now a screenwriter. As I've mentioned, this is a very personal process. As such, I encourage you to make it your own. Following this method to the letter is only one way to do it. This way has worked for me and I wanted to share it with you. If you feel like a part of the process doesn't work for you, I encourage you to modify, move, or skip it altogether. What I hope that I have provided you with here is simply a box of tools for you to build with. If you don't see the need for one or more of those tools, I won't be offend-ed. In all honesty, many screenwriting books are lucky if they impart one or two pieces of useful wisdom. I hope that is not the case with this book. Even if it is, I hope those pieces of wisdom serve you well. There are as many ways to write a screenplay as there are screenwriters. With this in mind, I'd like to recap some of the parts of the process that I feel are most important.

Finish: It's simple. If you don't finish, you have nothing. A partially written script is nothing. It can't be read. It can't be submitted to a screenplay contest. It can't be made into a film. A bad finished script can be improved. A good unfinished script is nothing. If you only take one thing from this whole book it is this: FINISH YOUR SCRIPT!

Don't edit until it is complete: Editing comes later. Don't stop. Your rough draft needs to be written in one giant, epic, uninterrupted blast of imagination. It needs to dump out of your mind onto the page. Creativity has to flow like a river. That flow doesn't happen if you are constantly stopping to go back and put in a dam. If you keep second guessing yourself as you write, you'll never finish. Once you have a rough draft, then you can go back and make changes. NEVER DURING.

Know your characters: Your characters are your movie. Story and plot are important but without characters that the audience cares about, they mean nothing. Working out every last little tedious detail in your characters cements them in your mind. After that comes everything else. How they fit into the plot, what they say, and how the audience can relate to them all become much easier after you know them. Make your characters real. You should know them, honor them, and protect them. I'll say it one last time: your characters are the most important part of your screenplay.

Make it personal: No one else in the history of humanity has lived your exact life. You are unique. Use this. Bring everything that you are to your screenplay. Extract everything you can from your personal experiences. Things you've done, seen, heard, overheard, learned about, or wanted are all fair game. All of those experiences are particular to your life. That's what can make your story interesting. That's what can be your reason to write. Your script should matter to you on a deep level. It should feel like you have to write it even if no one understands your reasoning. It's your little secret. A secret you share with only the page in front of you.

Keep going: I'm always writing something. Always. Your creativity is just like a muscle: flex it often and it will grow stronger. You can't stop because you feel discouraged. Don't compare yourself to others. Don't worry about a time frame. Just keep writing. As author Richard Bach once said, "A professional writer is an amateur who didn't quit." This is completely true. There is no invisible line between real writers and amateurs, except quitting. Don't diminish yourself by saying you're not a "real" writer. Don't demean your work when speaking to others about it. Don't say you just "like to write." If you are putting words on paper on a regular basis, you are a writer. Period. Own it. Don't be ashamed of it. Use it. Keep going. Just write.

Screenwriter William Goldman famously said of writing, "Nobody knows anything." What I think he meant was that there aren't *really* any rules to writing. There's no one way to do it. Therefore, no one knows the perfect way, because it doesn't exist. With that in mind, I hope that you've learned *a way* to do it. At least for the first time. What I hoped to do with this book is to take some of the fear or confusion away from those who wish to write but found the idea too complex or too massive. I hope you've gained some confidence, some know-how, and some motivation. Whatever way you get it done, I'm glad you're taking that first step.

A big part of that first step is reading this book. In the beginning, I said you've come to the right place. I hope you also believe that now. There are many places you can go to learn about screenwriting, so I am so happy that you have chosen the one I have assembled. I genuinely hope that this book serves as a stepping stone to a long and fruitful screenwriting career for you. One that includes many more screenplays, awards, and films hitting the silver screen with your name on them. Until then, I'll just say thanks again for letting me guide you through Your First Screenplay.

Appendix A

Character History

CHARACTER NAME:

GENERAL

Date this chart was completed:

Character's Full Name:

Reason or meaning of name:

Nickname:

Reason for nickname:

Birthdate:

Astrological Sign:

Where does character live?

       With anyone? (Yes/No) Who?

Where does character want to live?

APPEARANCE

Age:

How old does s/he appear?

Height:

Weight:

Type of body/build:

Eye color:

Glasses or contacts?

Hair Color:

Distinguishable hair feature (bald, receding hairline, etc.):

Type of hair (coarse, fine, thick, etc.):

Typical hairstyle:

Typical style of dress (formal, shabby, vintage, etc.):

Jewelry?
Other accessories?
Nationality:
Skin tone:
Shape of face:
Distinguishing Marks/Scars:
Most predominant feature:
Resembles (famous or not):
Accent?
Is s/he healthy?
        If not, why not?
Physical disabilities:
Physical abilities (what is character good at? Sports, etc.):

GOALS

What does character want most in the world?
What are they willing to do to get it?
Immediate goal(s):
Long term goal(s):
How does character plan to accomplish goals?
How will other people around character be affected?

FAVORITES

Color:
Music:
Movie:
Food:
Most prized possession?
        Why?
Expression:
Book:
Quote:
Expletive(s) (swears):
Mode of transportation:

Does character like animals? (Yes/No) Any pets?

HABITS

Spending habits (frugal, etc.):

What does s/he do too much of?

Too little of?

Smokes?

> What?
>
> How often?

Drinks?

> What?
>
> How often?

Worst bad habit:

Best good habit:

BACKGROUND

Hometown:

Type of childhood:

First memory:

Most important childhood event that still affects him/her:

> Why?

Lower education:

Higher education:

Booksmart or streetsmart?

Religion and/or religious views:

Firsts:

> Job?
>
> Kiss?
>
> Sexual Experience?

FAMILY

Mother's name:

> Relationship with her:

Father's name:

Relationship with him:
Number of siblings (brothers/sisters):
   Birth order:
   Relationship with each:
Children of siblings:
Extended family (aunts, uncles, cousins, etc.):
Close to family? Yes/No
Does character have children? Yes/No
   How many?
Are all children with the same partner?
   If no, why not?
   If no, what is custody arrangement?
How does character relate to his/her children?
Which child is character's favorite?
   Why?
Character's most favorite memory of his/her children?
Character's least favorite memory of his/her children?
Is relationship with children good?
Is relationship with children important to character?

JOB
Where does character work?
   How many years?
Relationship with co-workers?
Likes his/her job?
   Why or why not?
Dream job:

ATTITUDE
Greatest fear:
What single event would most throw character's life into complete turmoil?

Character is most at ease when:

Most ill at ease when:
Personal philosophy:
Self-esteem level? Low/Medium/High
Past failure s/he would be embarrassed to have people know about:

If granted one wish, what would it be?
    Why?
Daredevil or cautious?
      Same when alone?
Biggest regret?
Biggest accomplishment:
Minor accomplishments:
Character's darkest secret:
      Does anyone else know?
      If yes, did character tell them?
      If no, how did they find out?

PERSONALITY

Greatest source of strength in character's personality (whether s/he sees it as such or not):

Greatest source of weakness in character's personality (whether s/he sees it as such or not):

Character's soft spot:
      Is soft spot obvious to others?
      If not, how does character hide it?
Biggest vulnerability:

Which of the seven deadly sins does the character fight (or give into, willingly or not)?
      lust, gluttony, greed, sloth, wrath, envy, pride

Which of the seven virtues does character have (or fight against)?
chastity, abstinence, charity, diligence, patience, humility, kindness

ATTRIBUTES
Is character intelligent?
What makes the character feel pleasure?
What makes the character feel pain?
Optimist or pessimist?
Introvert or extrovert?
Drives and motivations:
Talents (hidden or not)?
Extremely skilled at:
Extremely unskilled at:
Good characteristics:
Character flaws:
Mannerisms/quirks:

PERCEPTION OF SELF
One word character would use to describe self:
One sentence description of how character would describe self:

What does character consider best physical characteristic?
What does character consider to be the worst physical characteristic?
Are these realistic assessments?
If not, why not?
How character thinks others perceive him/her:
What three things would character most like to change about self (#1 most important etc.):
#1:
#2:
#3:
If #1 change was made, would character be as happy as s/he thinks?

RELATING WITH OTHERS
What type of person is character attracted to?
Is character divorced? Why?

      If yes, how many times?

Has character ever cheated on any significant other?
How does character relate to others?
Is character good at giving and/or taking advice?
How is s/he perceived by...

      Strangers?

      Friends?

      Wife/Husband/Lover?

      Children?

      Co-workers?

      Protagonist?

      Antagonist?

First impression character make is:

      What happens to change this perception?

What do family/friends like most about character?
What do family/friends like least about character?
Who is the character's personal hero?
Person character secretly admires:
Person character was most influenced by:
Most important person in character's life before story starts:

      Why?

CRISIS RESPONSE
How character reacts in a crisis (calm, panic, etc.):
How does character face problems (head on, avoid, etc.)?

      Kinds of problems character usually runs into:

How does character react to new problems?
How does character react to change?

TECHNICAL
Does character know how to drive?

Do they own a car? (Yes/No) If yes, what kind?
Play musical instrument?

      Which one(s)?

Does character use computers? (Yes/No)

      If yes, what devices do they have (phone, tablet, etc.)?

Does character use social media? (Yes/No)

      If yes, are they proficient at it?

      Do they enjoy it? Or is it an obligation?

Appendix B

Recommended Screenplays (and movies)

12 Monkeys (1995)

Adaptation (2002)

A Few Good Men (1992)

Apocalypse Now (1979)

Atonement (2007)

The Aviator (2004)

Back to the Future (1985)

Beginners (2010)

Being John Malkovich (1999)

Big Fish (2003)

The Big Lebowski (1998)

Blade Runner (1982)

Brick (2005)

Casablanca (1942)

Children of Men (2006)

Chinatown (1974)

Citizen Kane (1941)

Closer (2004)

Die Hard (1988)

Dog Day Afternoon (1975)

Eternal Sunshine of the Spotless Mind (2004)

Ex Machina (2014)

Fargo (1996)

Fight Club (1999)

Forrest Gump (1994)

The French Connection (1972)

The Godfather (1972)

The Godfather: Part II (1974)
Goodfellas (1990)
Good Will Hunting (1997)
The Graduate (1967)
Hell or High Water (2016)
His Girl Friday (1940)
In Bruges (2008)
Inception (2010)
Jarhead (2005)
Jaws (1975)
L.A. Confidential (1997)
Layer Cake (2004)
The Lighthouse (2019)
Lost in Translation (2003)
The Maltese Falcon (1941)
Marriage Story (2019)
Memento (2000)
Michael Clayton (2010)
Miller's Crossing (1990)
Minority Report (2002)
Moonstruck (1987)
Mystic River (2003)
Network (1976)
No Country for Old Men (2007)
One Flew Over the Cuckoo's Nest (1975)
Parasite (2019)
Pulp Fiction (1994)
Raging Bull (1980)
Raiders of the Lost Ark (1981)
Rear Window (1954)
Reservoir Dogs (1992)
The Royal Tenenbaums (2001)
Se7en (1995)
The Shape of Water (2017)

The Shawshank Redemption (1994)
Sideways (2004)
The Silence of the Lambs (1991)
The Social Network (2010)
Star Wars (1977)
Taxi Driver (1976)
There Will Be Blood (2007)
Three Billboards Outside Ebbing, Missouri (2017)
Three Kings (1999)
The Truman Show (1998)
Unforgiven (1992)
The Usual Suspects (1995)
Wonder Boys (2000)
You Can Count On Me (2000)

About the Author

Adam Fiske is an acclaimed screenwriter and director. His films have won awards in film festivals all over the world, including in France, England, Italy, Japan, Spain, and Brazil. After writing his first feature screenplay at age 19, he continued writing features throughout the next two decades. These scripts resulted in successes in multiple prestigious contests including ScreenCraft Screenwriting Fellowship, The Writer's Store Spotlight Competition, and Scriptapalooza among many others. He does script consulting, releases films, and develops projects through his company Image Machine. He currently resides in Southern California.

Did you find this book helpful? If so, I'd love to hear about it. Honest reviews help readers like yourself find the right book for their needs.

Printed in Great Britain
by Amazon

43311731R00106